DIARY OF DEMOCRACY

The Story of Political Parties in America

Through the years the governing processes in the United States have undergone constant change, but nowhere is that change more graphically and dramatically reflected than in the political parties formed by the people to give voice to their opinions. This thorough and highly readable study of the rise and fall of political parties in America, brings to life important persons, events and issues that are a significant part of the great drama of a free people engaged in the difficult task of self-government.

BOOKS BY HARRY EDWARD NEAL

INFORMATIONAL

COMMUNICATIONS
From Stone Age to Space Age

DIARY OF DEMOCRACY
The Story of Political Parties in America

FROM SPINNING WHEEL TO SPACECRAFT
The Story of the Industrial Revolution

MONEY

THE MYSTERY OF TIME

THE PROTECTORS
The Story of the Food and Drug Administration

SIX AGAINST CRIME
Treasury Agencies in Action

THE TELESCOPE

TREASURES BY THE MILLIONS
The Story of the Smithsonian Institution

CAREERS

ENGINEERS UNLIMITED
Your Career in Engineering

DISEASE DETECTIVES
Your Career in Medical Research

NATURE'S GUARDIANS
Your Career in Conservation

SKYBLAZERS
Your Career in Aviation

YOUR CAREER IN ELECTRONICS

YOUR CAREER IN THE FOREIGN SERVICE

DIARY OF DEMOCRACY

The Story of Political Parties in America

BY HARRY EDWARD NEAL

Julian Messner   *New York*

Published simultaneously in the United States and Canada by
Julian Messner, a division of Simon & Schuster, Inc.,
1 West 39 Street, New York, N.Y. 10018. All rights reserved.

Copyright © 1970, 1962 by Harry Edward Neal

Photographs used with the permission
of the Library of Congress; Harris & Ewing

Printed in the United States of America
ISBN-0-671-32292-3 Cloth Trade
32293-1 MCE
Library of Congress Catalog Card No. 70-124304

INTRODUCTION

As Artemus Ward, a famous American humorist, once wrote, "I am not a politician—and my other habits are good."

The maneuvering, the jockeying, the wheeling-and-dealing, as well as the difficult decisions and enormous responsibilities that have been part of many political careers, make me content to be a voter and a writer. It has been said that politics is the art of getting money from the rich and votes from the poor by promising to protect one from the other; but politics and politicians are vital to the preservation of our government as we know it, and I have tried to show this in the pages ahead.

In my research for this book I learned many fascinating things about our American political system, its origins, growth and development. Unfortunately some historians recorded dates and versions of events which are at variance with those given by others, and I have tried to sort out those which a consensus indicated to be accurate.

Also, historians differ as to the significance and meanings of various political aims and moves. I have provided the facts as I found them, to present as impartial an account as possible.

I have not attempted to write the entire history of the United States, because my book is primarily about American political parties; but I have tried to sort out events of major political significance and to show their effects upon parties. The Civil War, for example, is mentioned briefly, but the political party activity that preceded and followed it is told in some detail; and this is the plan of the book wherever other pertinent historical events took place.

The story is told in chronological order to show the course of history and political events, many of which prove that in politics, as in other fields, we can learn a great deal by what has gone before.

My profound thanks go to Miss Roy Land, of the Alderman Library in the University of Virginia, founded by Thomas Jefferson in Charlottesville, for her gracious assistance in making research material available to me. For other information or helpful suggestions I am also indebted to the Republican National Committee, the Democratic National Committee, The League of Women Voters, The American Political Science Association of Washington, D. C.—and to my representative in Congress, Mr. Howard W. Smith.

As in all of my other books, I have tried hard to make this one enjoyable to read, as well as informative.

HARRY EDWARD NEAL

CONTENTS

CHAPTER		PAGE
	Introduction	5
1	Whigs, Tories and Revolution	11
2	Parties of the First Part	21
3	Aliens, Electors and the War of 1812	37
4	Compromise, Calhoun and "Old Hickory"	50
5	Tippecanoe and Bigots, Too	70
6	Republicans and Rebellion	86
7	Carpetbags, Ladies and Tammany Hall	99
8	Blaine, Bryan and "Dollar Mark" Hanna	116
9	From Teddy Roosevelt to Teapot Dome	130
10	The Big Slump, The New Deal and "Ike"	145
11	The Coming of The New Frontier	164
	Suggested Further Readings	181
	Index	183

DIARY OF DEMOCRACY

The Story of Political Parties in America

CHAPTER

1

WHIGS, TORIES AND REVOLUTION

November 11, 1620: Today the good ship Mayflower, Virginia-bound from Plymouth, England, with 102 souls aboard, anchored off Cape Cod, far from the land for which her passengers hold a charter from the Virginia Company. Since their charter is not binding upon this land, they have drawn up an unusual Compact as a guide by which they shall govern themselves.

March 22, 1765: The British Parliament has enacted a new law, the Stamp Act, to compel the American colonies to buy tax stamps for some 55 different articles. The colonists have no spokesmen in Parliament and are so justly angered by this taxation without representation that the Whigs intend to fight it. The Tories, however, side with the King.

July 4, 1776: The colonists' break with England was made official today by a formal Declaration of Independence signed at Philadelphia. Actually we have been at war with the British since the Minute Men clashed with them at Lexington on April 18 last year. Our cause is just. We fight for liberty, and with God's help we will win.

THE Mayflower Compact was simply a pledge of the Pilgrims to govern themselves, and has been called the basis for "the first pure democracy in the world." In it they vowed to "enacte, constitute, and frame such just & equall laws, ordinances, acts, constitutions, and offices, from time to time, as shall be thought most meete & convenient for ye generall good of ye Colonie unto which we promise all due submission and obedience."

After a month at Provincetown the *Mayflower* sailed further down the coast to Plymouth, where the Pilgrims founded what became the Massachusetts Bay Colony. In the years ahead the Colony became a haven for thousands of Pilgrims who fled persecution in England and looked to America as a land of freedom and promise.

Freedom and promise were not easily found. Governed by John Winthrop, the Massachusetts Bay Colony was a theocracy, or "Bible commonwealth," in which church and state were one, and any man, woman or child who did not choose to live by the strict Puritan rules was not welcome. In other words, many of those who crossed the seas in search of religious, economic and political freedom found only a new brand of religious tyranny under narrow, bigoted leaders.

For example, a colonist named John Oldham cried out that the Colony was controlled by "proprietors" in England who had never seen the New World, knew nothing of its real problems, and cared even less. For such accusations Oldham was convicted of the crime of sedition—creating discontent—and of profaning the church. He was sentenced to be publicly shamed and banished forever.

In the execution of this sentence the authorities stood Oldham before two lines of Pilgrim musketeers who raised their guns like clubs and waited expectantly. It is recorded that Oldham was "compelled in scorne to pass along betweene, and to receave a bob upon the bumme by every musketeir. And then aboard a shallop [a small boat] and so conveyed to Wessaguscus shore."

Oldham went to Watertown on the Charles River, where he found people with broader minds and a true democratic spirit. In 1634, with the town's founders, Sir Richard Saltonstall and the Reverend George Phillips, Oldham sponsored a free election for a Board of Selectmen—a governing group chosen of, by, and for the townspeople. This was the first body of its kind in all New England, a forerunner of a democratic national government.

In desperation other people deserted the Massachusetts Bay Colony and traveled to what are now the states of Connecticut and Rhode Island to establish new beachheads and more democratic governments.

Other British colonies were set up along the coast under three different types of government: Royal, Charter and Proprietary. In each a royal governor or a "proprietor" was the leader, but the people elected their own representatives in at least one house of the legislature, and it was by such public service that many men acquired the training and knowledge that later helped to build a strong America.

Among the colonists there were differences of opinion about taxes, budgets, schools, local laws or ordinances, and other matters affecting the lives of the people. Although there were no *organized* political parties it was natural that with these problems and three kinds of colonial governments people would take sides.

In England, where political differences also existed, two "parties" had opposite views about the proposed accession of James, Duke of York, to the English throne. One group, called "Whigs," fought against the accession because James had adopted the Roman Catholic faith and they wanted a Protestant king. The other faction, known as "Tories," took the view that James was entitled to the crown by virtue of royal succession and that he should have it regardless of his church affiliation or religious beliefs.

In other words, the Whigs believed they should have power to keep an undesirable king from being crowned, and the

Tories insisted that the royal blood line should be observed under any circumstances.

There are different versions of the origin of the name-calling terms "Whig" and "Tory." One is that "Whig" came from the Scottish colloquial name "Whiggamore," meaning a herdsman (similar to the American cowboy). As a term of ridicule the herdsmen were accused of living on sour whey, or "whig," a common drink, and it was in derision that the colonists who favored self-government were called "Whigs" by their opponents.

"Tory" allegedly came from the Irish word *Toree*, meaning "give me," which was used by Irish robbers in confronting their victims. One scholar, however, believed that the term could be traced to Irish supporters of Charles II during the Cromwell era, whose byword, *Tar-a-Ri* (pronounced *toree*), meant "Come, O King." Another said that the name was derived from *toringhim*, meaning "to chase for the sake of plunder," and that it was applied to certain Irishmen who refused to submit to Cromwell.

The shiploads of colonists coming to America from England brought with them their political ideas and convictions, with the result that the first "parties" in the New World bore the same names as in the Old—Whigs (liberals) and Tories (royalists). They were not organized as are political parties today, and for many years their influence upon government was small, since they were all subjects of His Royal Majesty, whose power made any vigorous opposition unwise.

In 1765, under George III, the British Parliament passed the Stamp Act, which would compel the colonies to pay for British government stamps to be placed on official papers, newspapers, books, playing cards, even on calendars. The money collected, said Parliament, would pay the costs of fighting the French and Indian War and of the military activity in the colonies.

Now, for the first time, there was a strong and sharp political division between the Whigs and Tories. The Tories were for the Stamp Act, the Whigs against it. Formal protests were made in some of the lower houses of the colonial legislatures. Opponents of the Stamp Act led movements to stop buying goods from England and to build up manufacturing in the colonies. When purchases declined, the British manufacturers began to suffer and took the side of the colonists to have the Act repealed.

Massachusetts invited representatives of the thirteen colonies to take part in a "Stamp Act Congress" in New York City. Nine of the colonies accepted, and this Congress sent England formal protests against the Stamp Act, but the House of Commons in London refused to consider the protests on the grounds that they came from a body without authority.

In Virginia's legislature, called the House of Burgesses, a member named Patrick Henry spoke out against the Act. Henry, then only twenty-nine years old, had been a storekeeper and a farmer, and had failed as both. In 1760 he began the study of law and in some six weeks became a member of the Virginia bar. Within five years his brilliant work in the courtroom helped to push him down the road to political fame. He became a member of the first Virginia Committee of Correspondence, and in 1765 when the Stamp Act was passed he was elected a member of the Virginia legislature.

In that position Henry wrote a number of resolutions calling for the colonies to rise against the Stamp Act, declaring that they had the right to make their own laws without interference from the British Parliament. His impassioned speech to the legislators about these resolutions was interrupted by cries of "Treason! Treason!"

Facing his fellow members, his voice strong and solemn, with upraised arm and a warning finger he said, "Caesar had his Brutus, Charles the First his Cromwell, and George the Third may profit by their example. If this be treason, make the most of it!"

Because of the bold and unexpected violent opposition to the Stamp Act throughout the colonies it was repealed by Parliament in 1766, but William Pitt, a brilliant English statesman, engineered the passage of a new law, the Declaratory Act, which gave England the right to make other laws that would "bind the colonies in all cases whatsoever." Since the colonists still had no representatives in Parliament, this Act made them inferior to other British subjects.

The American victory over the Stamp Act had two important results: It created a national feeling that united the colonists, and it set smoldering a political tinderbox that was to burst into flames of rebellion. Now the Whigs and Tories drew well-defined lines. The Whigs were the American patriots. The Tories were the English sympathizers.

New British laws met more opposition in the colonies, where the desire for true self-government was growing stronger. On December 16, 1773, a group of Boston patriots, dressed as Indians, dumped 342 chests of British tea into Boston Harbor. The British then enacted the Boston Port Bill, which would close Boston to all commercial shipping until the colonists paid for their "tea party."

The Virginia legislature held a day of prayer and fasting on June 1, 1774, when the Boston Port Bill was to take effect, and the royal governor promptly ordered the lawmakers to close down. Other colonial legislatures were also dissolved by royal order. The Virginians then proposed that representatives of the colonies meet in a congress in Philadelphia to consider their problems.

On September 5, 1774, the Continental Congress held its first session. Some members were in favor of compromises with the king, but others called for active resistance. The latter included Patrick Henry, who declared, "The distinctions between Virginians, Pennsylvanians and New Englanders are no more. I am not a Virginian, but an American!"

Also in 1774, in New York City, a young college student stood listening to speakers at a mass meeting shouting about the growing differences between England and the colonies. Fired by a feeling that their arguments were not strong enough, the youth elbowed his way through the crowd, climbed to the platform, made a stirring speech for colonial rights and was cheered and applauded by the listeners.

"What's your name, lad?" someone asked.

"Alexander Hamilton," he said.

Hamilton was born January 11, 1757, on Nevis Island in the British West Indies. His father was shiftless and deserted his family when Hamilton was about eight years old. His mother taught her son as best she could and eventually sent him to St. John's School in the islands, where he took a keen interest in arithmetic and business subjects. When he was eleven he was hired as an apprentice clerk in a mercantile firm, and at about this time his mother died. The courts gave her property to Peter Levine, Hamilton's half-brother, leaving Alexander without a penny.

When he was fourteen Hamilton met the Reverend Hugh Knox, a Presbyterian minister, who was so impressed by the boy's brilliance that he collected funds from friends and sent him to a school in New Jersey from which Hamilton later went to King's College (Columbia University) in New York City. It was at this time that he thrilled the crowd by his speech at the mass meeting.

This episode plunged him headlong into the controversy. Anonymously he wrote and published two pamphlets which the public acclaimed and attributed to well-known patriots, and when it was discovered that they were the work of a seventeen-year-old, Hamilton found himself classed as a youthful leader in the colonial cause.

On April 18, 1775, a troop of British soldiers exchanged shots with armed "Minute Men" at Lexington, Massachusetts, and the thirteen colonies were finally at war with Great Britain.

Officially the colonists broke with England by making a formal "Declaration of Independence." Primarily the work of Thomas Jefferson, this document incorporated the first formal term "United States of America" and set out the reasons for taking up arms against the king.

When the Declaration of Independence was adopted by the Second Continental Congress on July 4, 1776, the relations between Whigs and Tories had become violent. The Whigs, who were in the majority, persecuted the Tories whenever possible. Tory lands were seized and their owners banished, with the result that thousands of Tories returned to England or emigrated to Canada. Thousands of others joined the British forces, helped to burn colonial towns and fought with the Indians against the American rebels.

In 1776 the Congress appointed a committee to draw up a suggested agreement to be entered into by the colonies for their own guidance until their differences with England were settled. The agreement was based upon recommendations made by Benjamin Franklin in 1775 and was sent to the states to be ratified, or approved, in 1777.

This agreement was known as the Articles of Confederation. Under these Articles the Continental Congress could set up a government, complete with army and navy, could enter into treaties with foreign powers, and was given certain other authority—but there was one big catch. It had no power to levy taxes or to raise money in other ways to operate the government! If money was needed the Congress could only ask that each state contribute a share, much like a "pass-the-hat" office collection. The real power rested with each state, and if one opposed or ignored any congressional "suggestion" there was nothing Congress could do about it. In other words, the Continental Congress was a political body without muscles.

During the war the states were fairly well unified, but when the war neared its end the small states were jealous of the big ones, and the planters and farmers were suspicious of the merchants and other businessmen.

"Watch out for those southern farmers!" the New Englanders said. "They'll want to run the country."

"Be careful about those New England manufacturers!" the farmers warned. "They'll want to run the country."

Some Americans were friendly to France, which supported the colonies during the Revolution, while others disliked the French and favored England, their native land.

Some thought there should be a strong central government, and others believed just as firmly that a strong central government would rob the states of their freedom and that each state should set up its own rights and privileges.

These were the major political issues when the Articles of Confederation were finally ratified in 1781.

Under George Washington's leadership the British were defeated in 1781, the thirteen colonies became thirteen "free and independent states . . . absolved from all allegiance to the British Crown," and the new nation prepared to seek the "life, liberty and pursuit of happiness" promised by the Declaration of Independence.

The battles of the Revolution had ended, but others were about to begin.

CHAPTER

2

PARTIES OF THE FIRST PART

September 17, 1787: This day marked a great and solemn moment in the history of our new nation, as General George Washington affixed the first signature to the Constitution of the United States at Independence Hall in Philadelphia. Holding a pen in one hand he stood up, looked at the hushed delegates and said, "Should the states reject this excellent Constitution, the probability is that an opportunity will never again be offered to cancel another in peace—the next will be drawn in blood!"

April 30, 1789: General Washington was sworn in today as the first President of the United States, and there was a lot of fanfare and fol-de-rol in New York. It is said that the general's Cabinet will include Alexander Hamilton and Thomas Jefferson, which is somewhat surprising, since Hamilton is a Federalist and Jefferson an Anti-Federalist. There are bound to be clashes, but both men are patriots and their political differences may help to keep things in good balance. Also, Washington will have John Adams as Vice President, and these two leaders aren't likely to stand for any rash actions.

THE shooting war ended in 1781, but a formal treaty of peace with England was not signed until 1783. The political war between Whigs and Tories continued, with the Tories on the losing end. Some were tarred and feathered and driven out of their communities. Some had their homes and belongings confiscated, some were jailed or forcibly returned to England, some were even put to death, depending upon the extent to which they had helped the British cause.

Because of jealousies and differences among the states, few laws were made under the Confederation. Each state had one vote. Nine states had to agree in order to pass a new law, and no changes could be made in the Articles of Confederation themselves without the unanimous approval of the states, which was practically impossible to obtain.

In 1783 the American army was disbanded, General Washington resigned as its commander and returned to his home in Mount Vernon, Virginia. As a group the Tories had vanished, so the Whigs were the only remaining political "party" in the country. The Whigs, however, had political differences among themselves. Those who favored strong state governments were called "Particularists" and those who preferred a powerful central government were known as "Strong Government" Whigs.

The country did not prosper in its new-found freedom. Continental currency was so worthless that Washington himself admitted a farmer needed a wagonload of money to buy a plow. Along the coast the merchants traded with privateers and smugglers who could pay in gold, but in the interior the people suffered. Flour sold for nearly $1600 a barrel. Butter was $12 a pound, corn $150 a bushel. Whole towns did business by barter, trading onions for turnips, cloth for flour, or labor for potatoes.

Farmers who owed money and could not pay had their homes and lands seized by their creditors and were also thrown into prison as debtors, then forced to "work off" what they still owed. The states imposed heavy taxes which most citizens couldn't pay.

War veterans were puzzled and disgruntled. "Is this what we fought for?" they asked. "What kind of freedom is this?"

"Aye—we were better off under the rule of the king," others said.

In 1786 in the backwoods of western Massachusetts, a former Revolutionary hero, Captain Daniel Shays, recruited bands of veterans called "The Regulators." Those who had no guns were armed with horsewhips, knives, swords or wooden clubs. Shays' plan was simple.

"Our people are being brought into court and sent to jail as debtors," he said. "We've petitioned our lawmakers for relief and gotten none. Now we'll make our own laws! We'll march into the towns and close the courts. No courts, no convictions, no more people in jail."

With his ragged, hungry army Shays invaded several Massachusetts towns. If they arrived when a court was in session they threw the presiding judge into the streets, locked the courtroom doors, broke open the local jail and freed the debtors.

Early in 1787 Shays' "army" consisted of more than 1200 men, and he conceived a bold plan to storm the Federal arsenal at Springfield, center of the government's military might. He would seize all the guns and ammunition, distribute them among his soldiers, then march into Boston and take over the state government.

Marshaling his forces on the outskirts of Springfield, Shays led them against the fortified arsenal. Its defenders fired an artillery volley over the heads of the attackers as a warning to halt, but the Shays men mistook its meaning.

"They're on our side!" someone shouted. "They're shootin' over our heads. Come on, boys, come on!"

Yelling and laughing they began to run up the hill on which the arsenal stood. Then came the crash of another volley, this time aimed directly into their ranks. A few men stumbled and fell. The others, startled and scared, dropped their guns and sticks and swords, turned and ran in all directions. Shays barked orders to stay and fight, but they went unheeded. Not one Regulator fired a shot.

Some of the rebels were caught and imprisoned, but later all of them, including Shays, were pardoned on the grounds that they were driven to revolt by economic circumstances which they could not endure.

The Shays Rebellion played an important part in American political history. On March 25, 1787, George Washington wrote a letter to the Marquis de Lafayette which told about the rebellion and said:

> These disorders are evident marks of a defective government; indeed the thinking people of this country are now so well satisfied of this fact that most of the legislatures have appointed—and the rest, it is said, will appoint—delegates to meet at Philadelphia the second Monday in May next, in a general Convention of the States to revise and correct the defects of the Federal system.

The meeting Washington mentioned was called by the Congress to patch up and strengthen the Articles of Confederation. Held in Philadelphia's Independence Hall, where the Declaration of Independence was signed, the gathering was presided over by General Washington and attended by state-chosen delegates including Benjamin Franklin, James Madison and Alexander Hamilton. Franklin, at eighty-one, was the oldest delegate, and Jonathan Dayton of New Jersey, twenty-six, the youngest. The delegates included lawyers, doctors, soldiers, teachers, ministers and storekeepers.

After discussions about the Shays Rebellion and the nation's future welfare the delegates decided not to try to revise the Articles of Confederation, but instead to set up a new democratic government to be ruled by the people and not by independent states. There were all kinds of arguments.

"We should scrap the Articles and crown our own king," some delegates suggested.

"No! We don't want another monarchy," others argued. "What we should do is revise the state boundaries so that every state is the same size."

"Size means nothing," one declared. "The important thing is to have a strong national government with one man at its head."

"Absolutely not! That would be practically the same as a king. What we should have is a committee to run the government—a committee of seven or so."

Thus the most important issue, and the one which brought the greatest division of opinion, was: "Shall we have a strong national government with power vested in the people, or shall the power rest with the individual states?"

One proposal, called "The Virginia Plan," consisted of fifteen resolutions, mostly written by James Madison. This plan provided for a national executive, a national judicial system, and two houses of the legislature, one lower, one upper. Members of the lower house would be chosen by the people, but those of the upper house would be nominated by state legislatures and then appointed by the lower house. Madison's proposals were modified later, but they became the basis for the great document that is the Constitution of the United States, and for this reason Madison has been called "The Father of the Constitution."

There were arguments about having members of the upper house chosen by those of the lower. The big states wanted representation strictly according to population. The small ones argued that any such plan would squeeze them to the point where only the large states would have the run of government.

To equalize the power, the delegates finally agreed upon what they called the "Connecticut Compromise"—a decision to establish a two-part Congress consisting of a House of Representatives and a Senate. In the lower house each state would be represented by congressmen elected by the people according to its population. In the Senate each state would have two members, regardless of population or size.

The Constitution was written on four big sheets of paper, 28¾ inches by 23⅝ inches, and consisted of 4543 words, including its thirty-nine signatures. The literary form of the final draft is generally believed to be the work of Gouverneur Morris of New York State, a member of the Continental Congress and later United States Minister to France.

Basically the Constitution established three major branches of government—the Legislative (Congress), the Judicial (Supreme Court and lower federal courts), and the Executive (the President).

In brief, the Preamble to the Constitution states clearly the purpose of the American government:

> We, the People of the United States, in Order to form a more perfect Union, establish Justice, insure domestic Tranquility, provide for the common defence, promote the general Welfare, and secure the Blessings of Liberty to ourselves and our Posterity, do ordain and establish this Constitution for the United States of America.

Submitted to the states for ratification, the proposed Constitution was supported by many, opposed by many. Now the first real *American* political parties took form. Those "Strong Government" Whigs who were in favor of the adoption of the Constitution and a strong national government were now called the "Federalists." Their "Particularist" opponents were the "Anti-Federalists."

Among the Federalists were Alexander Hamilton, James Madison and John Jay. The Anti-Federalists included such men as Patrick Henry, Samuel Adams and Thomas Jefferson, who became the leader of the Anti-Federalist or "States' Rights" party.

The Anti-Federalists believed that the power of government should rest with the states and that an elected President, as proposed in the Constitution, would become as much of a tyrant as any king.

Despite strong opposition, one by one the states ratified the Constitution in this order: Delaware, Pennsylvania, New Jersey, Georgia, Connecticut, Massachusetts, Maryland, South Carolina, New Hampshire, Virginia and New York. As soon as the ninth state, New Hampshire, had ratified (June 21, 1788), the Constitution became binding.

The Constitutional Convention set March 4, 1789, as the date on which the new Constitution would take effect, and officially this is the date on which the old Confederation of States died, but not until April 6 were there enough members present for Congress to become active.

In considering a candidate for the Presidency, the name uppermost in the minds of all the people of the United States was that of George Washington, who had led them to victory in the Revolution. There was no political campaign, no statement of aims and principles, no opposition, and Washington was called from retirement to become the first chosen leader of the new nation.

Washington's inauguration on April 30, 1789, was a cause

for celebration. The people of New York City, which was then the nation's capital, paraded in the streets. Taverns and lodging houses were filled, and many visitors lived in tents pitched on open ground about the city. Hundreds of rowboats and sailboats swarmed in the Hudson River, and long lines of horse-drawn wagons and coaches rumbled into New York from nearby communities.

At noon a troop of cavalry, together with infantrymen and a company of Scottish Highlanders, escorted Washington through wildly cheering crowds to Federal Hall at Broad and Wall Streets.

The oath of office was administered by Chancellor Robert R. Livingston, who held a Bible open at the fiftieth chapter of Genesis as the general laid his hand upon the page. When the oath was given, Washington bowed and kissed the Bible as he said, "I swear, so help me God!"

"It is done," the chancellor said. Turning to the crowd he shouted, "Long live George Washington, President of the United States!"

The chancellor's cry was an echo of the English "Long live the King!" and it was not used again. There was, however, some disagreement about a proper title for the President. The Senate preferred "His Highness, the President of the United States and Protector of Their Liberties," and someone even suggested "His Mightiness," but the House of Representatives argued that this sounded too much like British royalty and suggested instead, "The President of the United States," as well as "The Vice President of the United States" for the second in command. The House won. The President was addressed as "Mr. President," although Washington himself preferred "Your Excellency."

The man chosen by the electors to be Vice President was John Adams, who took his oath of office on June 3. He was not the candidate of any political party, since there were not yet any strongly organized groups.

When Washington assembled his Cabinet in 1789 he appointed thirty-two-year-old Alexander Hamilton as Secretary of the Treasury, a move that laid the foundation for a sound central government, breathed life into the new Constitution, and paved the way for the formation of two organized American political parties.

Hamilton was short (5 feet 7 inches), slender, and walked with his shoulders back and his chin high, giving him both a cocky and dignified air. His reddish-brown hair was powdered and braided in a queue in the fashion of the times, and in his well-fitted clothes, from white silk stockings to ruffled lace jabot, he looked every inch an aristocrat. He was egotistical, vain and domineering, yet he was also generous, affectionate, courageous, persistent, thoroughly honest, eloquent, and a brilliant planner and writer. His conflicting traits won friends and created enemies, especially in the blossoming world of national politics. An important figure in that world and in Hamilton's career was Thomas Jefferson.

Born in what was called the "back country" near Charlottesville, Virginia, in 1743, Jefferson had very little early schooling. In his youth, like George Washington, he became a surveyor, but he was so eager for more education that he spent every spare hour in studies that would prepare him for college. He was admitted to William and Mary College, where he specialized in mathematics, botany, music and languages. He learned Spanish, Italian, Latin, Greek and French, became an excellent violinist and such a capable architect that he designed his own beautiful home at Monticello, where he conducted numerous experiments in farming and botany.

After graduation Jefferson studied law and for some years was a practicing attorney, becoming more and more interested in politics. In 1769 at the age of twenty-six he was elected to the Virginia House of Burgesses. As the conflict grew between England and the colonies, so did Jefferson's participation in it. He was elected to the Continental Congress in 1775 and 1776, drafted the Declaration of Independence, served as Governor of Virginia from 1779 to 1781, and in 1785 was appointed Minister to France. He returned to the United States in 1789 and in 1790 President Washington chose Jefferson to be his Secretary of State.

Jefferson was tall, lanky and rawboned, with red hair and blue eyes. Unlike Hamilton he did not dress in the height of fashion and often his plain clothes, worn in a careless manner, seemed to be one or two sizes too small for his six-foot frame.

As a politician and organizer Jefferson had no equal in his day. Where Hamilton had little concern for the people in general and held the viewpoint of the aristocrat, Jefferson believed that the true strength of the nation was to be found among the farmers, the mechanics, the carpenters and woodworkers of the back country. Most of these were loosely organized in factions in their own communities and were concerned with political developments in their towns and states. Jefferson decided that if they could be welded into one big party, concerned with both national *and* state politics, they would exert tremendous influence in the political future of the country.

In the various states Jefferson selected men qualified to act as leaders in building local party organizations. Not the least of these was John Pintard, chief of the Society of the Sons of Tammany in New York City. Originally Tammany was a non-partisan fraternal organization, but its members soon went all out for Jefferson and his party.

The Tammany Society grew from "Saint Tammany Clubs" which were active before and during the Revolution. "Tammany" was a distortion of "Tammanend," the name of a Delaware Indian chief who loved freedom, and the St. Tammany Clubs were organized to combat the Tories. After the war the clubs disbanded and the Tammany Society took their place. Each of its thirteen leaders was a "sachem" and their meeting place, Tammany Hall, was "The Wigwam." Tammany's support of Jefferson gave his party considerable strength in New York City.

Alexander Hamilton, too, had power. In Washington's administration he was a one-man "brain trust." As Secretary of the Treasury, the economic future of the new nation was in his hands, and in 1790 he sent to Congress his first "Report on the Public Credit," a masterful plan that started the United States on the road to prosperity and power.

Part of this plan called for the assumption of states' debts. That is, the national government would assume responsibility for paying the debts incurred by the states during the Revolution. There was tremendous resistance to this move. Some of Hamilton's opponents argued that the wealthy speculators in the northern states would buy up certificates from the southern states, while the people of the South would be unfairly taxed by the government to pay off the certificate holders.

The proposal was defeated in the House by two votes, but Hamilton was not discouraged. Not yet.

It happened that Congress was also battling about a permanent location for the national capital, which was then in New York City. Thomas Jefferson wanted the capital located on the Potomac River at Georgetown. New Englanders and New Yorkers wanted it to remain in New York. Some wanted it in eastern Pennsylvania.

Hamilton didn't care *where* the capital was located. His main interest was in getting enough votes in another effort to swing passage of his bill. With this in mind he approached Jefferson and discussed a bargain. If Jefferson would persuade certain Virginia congressmen to change their votes in favor of assumption, Hamilton would move to have the capital located on the Potomac.

Jefferson then brought Hamilton and James Madison together to discuss this proposition. Madison agreed to let the bill for assumption go to the House again with an amendment from the Senate, although he himself said he would not vote in favor of it.

To nail down the choice of the permanent location for the capital they would need votes of some Pennsylvania congressmen, so it was agreed that the capital would be located in Philadelphia for ten years, while the new city (Washington) was made ready to become the seat of the national government.

The bill for assumption was passed, thus sealing the Hamilton–Jefferson bargain and concluding the first major "logrolling" deal between leaders of the principal political parties.

Proceeding with the plan for a strong central government, Hamilton now proposed to set up a national bank patterned after the Bank of England. His opponents, led by Jefferson and Madison, protested that the Constitution did not authorize Congress to establish a national banking system and that to do so would be an abuse of power.

Hamilton's answer was that the necessary power was *implied* in the Constitution, which must be interpreted broadly and liberally.

The industrial North favored the bank. The agricultural South believed the bank would center the country's wealth in the northern states and hurt the southern planters.

When the Federalist Congress passed the bank bill, President Washington was cautious about signing it into law. But after hearing all arguments, including Hamilton's and Jefferson's, he decided that the proposed bank would benefit all of the people and he signed the bill, giving Hamilton another victory. Now, however, Hamilton and Jefferson were at political swords' points and the lines of political party warfare were clearly drawn.

When the country prospered under Hamilton's Federalist financial policies (his Bank of the United States was a great success), the Anti-Federalists felt that the very name of their party was losing them the support of many people who were now in sympathy with the Federalist government and its ideas. Although Jefferson and his Anti-Federalists supported the Constitution, they continued their opposition to Hamilton and his schemes and decided to form a new party which would fight any future moves by the government to assume powers that were not expressly authorized by the Constitution.

This new party joined forces with the local groups organized by Jefferson, and in 1792 he gave his followers the name of "Republicans." They were the "strict constructionists," advocating a strict interpretation of the language of the Constitution, thus limiting the powers of the national government. Their adversaries, the Federalists, were "loose constructionists," insisting that the powers granted by the Constitution must be interpreted in the broadest sense.

While Jefferson and Hamilton fought each other bitterly in print and elsewhere, a revolution that broke out in France in 1789 now broadened into a war between France on one side and Spain, Austria and England on the other. Hamilton had no sympathy with the French, was anxious to support the British. Jefferson considered the French our friends, the British our enemies. Washington refused to take sides and issued a proclamation of neutrality.

The personal conflict between Jefferson and Hamilton became so bitter that in 1793 Jefferson resigned as Secretary of State and retired to his home in Charlottesville, where he formulated plans for building a stronger major political party.

President Washington himself was roundly attacked in many quarters, was denounced by some as a British ally and a weakling, and was thoughtlessly smeared by people who once cheered him as the fearless warrior who had won America's independence.

Seeing an opportunity to grab political power in this conflict, groups of politicians formed "Democratic Clubs" modeled after similar clubs in France, and called the club members "Democrats."

The Jeffersonian Republicans did not formally affiliate with these Democratic Clubs, but did accept them as allies against the Federalists until Washington publicly branded the clubs as enemies of the whole American government. The Republicans then severed all ties with the clubs, which soon faded from the political scene.

In the political field, party organizations were growing in importance. In Washington's second administration only members of the Federalist party were appointed to government jobs. The Federalists were riding high—until Washington informed them in 1796 that he would not be a candidate for a third term. This threw them into a minor panic, for they had no one who could match Washington's influence as a vote-getter.

After considerable discussion the Federalists decided upon John Adams as their Presidential candidate, and Thomas Pinckney of South Carolina for the Vice Presidency.

The Republicans chose Thomas Jefferson and Aaron Burr as the opposing team.

At that time the candidate receiving the greatest number of electoral votes became President, and the one with the second highest number became Vice President. When the electoral votes were counted John Adams won the Presidency, but the number two man was Adams' powerful political opponent, Thomas Jefferson!

John Adams, like his predecessor, George Washington, was opposed to the creation of organized political parties. Adams declared that "the greatest political evil under the Constitution" was "the division of the Republic into two great parties, each under its leader."

In his farewell address upon leaving the Presidency in 1796, George Washington said:

> Let me . . . warn you in the most solemn manner against the baneful effects of the Spirit of Party, generally . . . .
> It serves always to distract the Public Councils and enfeeble the public administration. It agitates the community with ill-founded jealousies and false alarms, kindles the animosity of one part against another, foments occasionally riot and insurrection. It opens the door to foreign influence and corruption, which find a facilitated access to the Government itself through the channels of party passions. Thus the policy and the will of one country are subject to the policy and will of another . . . .

Although the differences of opinion about the Constitution and government policies established the line between the Federalists and the Jeffersonian Republicans, these groups were not yet strongly organized. With brilliant leadership, however, they would soon emerge as powerful political parties.

CHAPTER

3

ALIENS, ELECTORS AND THE WAR OF 1812

June 1, 1798: Our military forces are growing in numbers and we are fighting an undeclared war with France. All this stems from the humiliation inflicted upon our emissaries by the "XYZ" affair, which shocked the whole country.

July 14, 1798: Today the Federalist Congress passed the Alien and Sedition Laws, which give the President the power of a dictator and threaten to launch a reign of terror in the United States.

October 21, 1803: Congress today ratified the treaty for the Louisiana Purchase. How the wind changes! Tom Jefferson, always a stickler for strict interpretation of the Constitution, claims that his authority for this purchase was implied in the Constitution. Before he became President he insisted that this business of "implied" authority was nonsense. Things evidently look different through the windows of The White House.

September 25, 1804: The states have ratified the Twelfth Amendment, which changes the way we elect our Presidents and Vice Presidents. This should forestall deadlocks such as that which tied Jefferson and Burr for the Presidency in the last election.

June 1, 1812: Congress has voted to fight the British, mostly because of British interference with our shipping. Calhoun and Clay, the "War Hawks," ought to be satisfied now. They did everything they could to bring us to the shooting stage.

PRESIDENT JOHN ADAMS was so short and fat that someone once suggested he be referred to as "His Rotundity." Despite his roly-poly figure and his aristocratic background, Adams was highly respected for his political wisdom, his courage and his great devotion to his country regardless of his personal political fortunes.

Adams had inherited from Washington the problem of keeping the United States out of the war in Europe, but new developments created new political headaches. The French considered America an ally of England and an enemy of France, so the French navy began to seize American ships and cargoes. The Jeffersonian Republicans, who sympathized with France, were not too critical of the French actions. The pro-British Federalists, however, were outraged and demanded that President Adams, leader of their party, move to show the insolent French that the United States had the backbone to fight for its rights.

Like Washington, Adams wanted to keep America at peace if possible, so he sent three men to Paris to talk about a peaceful settlement of differences. Two were Federalists—John Marshall and Charles C. Pinckney. The third, Elbridge Gerry, was a Jeffersonian Republican.

The new French Foreign Minister, Talleyrand, insulted the American emissaries by refusing to meet them personally, and appointed three representatives to carry on "informal" discussions.

The discussions took a surprising turn. The French agents said, in effect, "We might consider negotiating with you—but for a price. Say, two hundred and fifty thousand dollars?"

The Americans stared at each other in disbelief. "What you propose is bribery!" one said. "We have no authority to pay any bribe."

When the Americans then attempted to talk about the French seizure of American ships, the French agents said,

"Gentlemen, you do not speak to the point. It is money. It is expected that you will offer money."

Charles Pinckney answered for his group. "The answer is no, no—not a sixpence!"

Later it was erroneously reported that Pinckney's words were, "Millions for defense, but not one cent for tribute!"

When Congress insisted upon a report about the mission to France, the President delivered all reports and correspondence concerning it, but identified the three French intermediaries only as "Agents X, Y and Z," and the documents later became known as the "XYZ dispatches."

Shocked by the story, Congress ordered the XYZ papers to be made public, and the whole country then clamored for retaliation against France. French-American treaties made in 1778 were declared annulled and Congress created a new and separate Navy Department and appropriated money to build new ships and recruit ten thousand fighting men. There was no formal declaration of war, but in reality a war between France and the United States began in 1798.

Something else that began in 1798 contributed to the downfall of the Federalist party. The Federalists had favored war with France and won public support that made the party stronger than its Jeffersonian Republican rivals. Capitalizing on the undeclared war and the feeling aroused by the XYZ papers, the Federalist-controlled Congress enacted new laws known as the "Alien and Sedition Acts." Supposedly the laws were aimed at French spies and agents in the United States, but many politicians believed that the real purpose was to weaken the Republicans by cutting down the political activity of pro-Republican Frenchmen in the United States.

The Alien Law required a foreigner to live in the United States for fourteen years before he could become an American citizen. It also authorized the President in peacetime to deport any alien he considered to be dangerous to the country, and gave the President the power during wartime to deport or jail any alien. Although these provisions were not enforced, they undoubtedly caused many French citizens living in the United States to hurry back to their own country.

The law that really backfired against the Federalists was the Sedition Act, which made it a crime for *anyone* to write or say anything about the President, the Senate, or the House of Representatives, that was "false, scandalous or malicious." (It was for an offense of this kind that John Oldham was banished by the bigots from the Massachusetts Bay Colony more than 150 years earlier.)

Several Republican newspaper editors who printed opinions criticizing the Federalist administration were arrested as violators of this law. Matthew Lyon, a congressman from Vermont, declared that President Adams was an aristocratic and selfish power-grabber whose foreign policies were faulty and harmful. Lyon was arrested, fined a thousand dollars and clapped into jail for four months.

When Anthony Haswell, another Vermonter, blasted the government for what he called its "political persecution" of Lyon, Haswell paid a two-hundred-dollar fine and served two months in prison.

On a visit to Newark, New Jersey, President Adams was honored by the firing of a salute from a battery of cannon. Gunpowder and cloth wadding were rammed through the gun muzzles, the order to fire was given, and the artillery thundered away. As the roar faded, a spectator, Luther Baldwin said jokingly, "I wish some of that wadding had hit Adams in the seat of the pants!"

A bystander who heard the remark reported it to the police,

who took Baldwin into custody and brought him before a judge who imposed a fine of one hundred dollars.

After several such incidents many people realized how oppressive the Sedition Act was, and in 1799 the question of its repeal came to a vote in Congress. The law was upheld. Jefferson and his Republicans strongly opposed Adams and the Federalists on this issue, and Jefferson drew up the "Kentucky Resolutions" which condemned the law. In Virginia another resolution drafted by James Madison declared that the national government had no right to enact legislation that affected free speech and a free press, and that such matters were for the states to decide.

While this battle was in progress, President Adams appointed a three-man commission to meet with the French. This meeting resulted in a new treaty of 1800 in which France promised to respect American neutrality and the United States agreed not to seek payment for American ships and cargoes captured by the French.

The French situation and the Alien and Sedition Laws were important political issues in the Presidential campaign of 1800. The Federalist candidates were John Adams for President and Charles C. Pinckney for Vice President. The Republican team was Thomas Jefferson and Aaron Burr. Thus Jefferson and Adams were opponents for the second time.

Some Federalists supported Adams while others, led by Alexander Hamilton, opposed him. Because of this internal conflict the Federalist party lost its unity. In addition, Adams fired his Secretaries of State and War, who were Hamilton's friends and supporters. Hamilton then denounced Adams in a confidential pamphlet which was supposed to be read only by certain influential Federalists. In this way Hamilton hoped that Pinckney would capture the Presidency, since Pinckney's ideas were in accord with Hamilton's. Unfortunately for Hamilton, his pamphlet fell into Republican hands and provided powerful ammunition for Adams' defeat and the election of Thomas Jefferson.

The Federalists, desperate to stir up opposition to the Republicans, criticized their program and began to call them "Democratic-Republicans" as a term of ridicule, a reminder of the Democratic Clubs which had been condemned earlier by George Washington.

Warranted or not, it was just such criticism and opposition that served to strengthen the two-party political system and the processes of democratic government.

Dissatisfied with the handling of the French situation and disgusted with the oppressive Alien and Sedition Laws, the voters defeated Adams and Pinckney but at the same time created a new political predicament. In the electoral college Thomas Jefferson and Aaron Burr each received seventy-three electoral votes for the Presidency, resulting in a deadlock that had to be broken by the House of Representatives.

In ballot after ballot Burr and Jefferson held the tie. Now Alexander Hamilton made one of the great decisions of his career. Although he was a bitter opponent of Jefferson, he considered Burr to be a corrupt and unscrupulous politician who would place his personal ambitions above good government. Jefferson, on the other hand, was an ardent patriot to whom the future of the nation was of first importance. Making his choice, Hamilton persuaded one congressman to abstain from voting, and on the thirty-sixth ballot Jefferson was elected, with Burr as Vice President. Hamilton's action not only defeated Burr, but also deepened Burr's resentment towards Hamilton.

Although the Federalists were voted out of office, they had

achieved a great deal in the interests of the nation. They had maintained a strong central government, refused alliances which would entangle the nation in the affairs of foreign countries and won international respect for the United States. Their greatest shortcoming was their inclination to favor those engaged in manufacturing and other commercial enterprises, and to neglect the farmers and workmen—the "common people," so important in a new democracy with expanding frontiers.

After Jefferson's inauguration the Republicans laid plans to change the electoral procedure. On December 12, 1803, a proposed Twelfth Amendment to the Constitution was submitted to Congress and on September 25, 1804, it was ratified by the states.

The Twelfth Amendment governs the operation of the electoral college, through which we elect our Presidents and Vice Presidents. This "college" has no campus, no dormitories, no faculty and bestows no degrees. It consists of all of the Presidential electors; and in each state there are as many electors as there are senators and representatives from that state.

Before the Twelfth Amendment the candidate who received the greatest number of votes in the electoral college became President, and the one who had the second highest number became Vice President. The Twelfth Amendment required *separate* votes for President and Vice President.

The votes of the electoral college as a whole govern the election of a President, and the political party that gets the *most* of a state's popular votes also gets *all* of its electoral votes. Under this system a Presidential candidate might receive more individual votes than his opponent and yet lose the election.

If a Presidential candidate fails to get a majority of electoral votes the election is decided in the House of Representatives by having each state cast a single vote for its choice, according to the wishes of the state delegation.

If the candidate for Vice President fails to get an electoral majority, the United States Senate chooses the Vice President, with each senator casting a single vote.

A candidate for the Presidency must be at least thirty-five years old, a native American citizen, and must have been a resident of the United States for at least fourteen years.

If the President dies he is succeeded by the Vice President. If there is no Vice President the line of succession to the Presidency begins with the Speaker of the House of Representatives, the President *pro tempore* (for the time being) of the Senate, and members of the Cabinet in the order of the dates on which their departments were created.

As our third President, Thomas Jefferson promised equal justice to all, encouraged farming and commerce, freedom of religion, press and individual, and other principles that were not likely to offend members of any political group. Where Washington and Adams had held formal receptions in The President's House, Jefferson announced that formality was abolished and that anyone could call at the house at any time. One morning when the fashionably dressed British Ambassador arrived to confer with the President on matters of state, he was surprised when Jefferson appeared in house slippers and shirt sleeves!

When Jefferson went into action as President, the country soon discovered that he meant business. With his Republican party in control of Congress he won repeal of the naturalization law and the excise tax on whiskey, and he pardoned all "offenders" who were convicted under the Alien and Sedition Acts, which expired in 1801.

In a bold move to protect American commerce the President obtained approval from Congress to spend not more than ten million dollars for the purchase of the French-owned New Orleans area and western Florida. He sent James Monroe overseas to work with Robert R. Livingston, our Minister to France, to negotiate with Talleyrand, representing Napoleon.

The negotiations were slow at first, but were climaxed by a surprise for the Americans. No, said Talleyrand, Napoleon would not sell New Orleans for a few million dollars—but he *would* sell the whole Louisiana territory for fifteen million! Take that or nothing.

Although they had no authority to spend so much money or to buy the whole territory, Monroe and Livingston decided to do so. (Western Florida was not included, since it belonged to Spain.) When Jefferson later learned of their action he was both startled and worried. As a "strict constructionist" Jefferson had always insisted that no liberties should be taken with the language of the Constitution, which meant exactly what it said and no more. This was a principle of his Republican followers, and they had severely criticized the Federalists for making broad and liberal interpretations of the Constitution.

Now the purchase of the Louisiana Territory created a political turnabout. Jefferson himself believed the purchase was not Constitutional and that the only solution was to amend the Constitution. His party argued that this would take too much time, that Napoleon might cancel his agreement, and that the whole matter should be presented to Congress for approval. This was done, and the Republicans boldly declared that the authority for the purchase was *implied* in the Constitution!

The Federalists promptly reversed their earlier position as "loose constructionists" and protested that there was no clearcut Constitutional authority for buying the land from France.

This complete switch pointed up one fact—*political principles and outlooks change according to the objectives of the party in power.*

There was considerable opposition from the Federalists in New England, who feared that acquisition of the new territory would weaken their economy and their political strength, but Congress ratified the treaty on October 21, 1803, and the United States took over nearly 828,000 square miles of land.

In 1804 Jefferson ran for re-election, but Aaron Burr, his first-term Vice President, had switched loyalties to become a Federalist candidate for the governorship of New York. Secretly Burr was involved in a plot conceived by a group of New England manufacturers who resented what they considered favoritism shown by the national government to agricultural interests. If Burr were elected governor he was to lead a bold move to have New York and New England secede from the Union.

When word of this plot reached Alexander Hamilton he exposed the whole scheme. Publicly disgraced, Burr challenged Hamilton to a duel. At seven o'clock on the morning of July 11, 1804, at Weehawken, New Jersey, Burr shot and mortally wounded Hamilton, who died the next day. He was forty-seven years old.

In 1808 came another Presidential election. Some of Jefferson's Republican followers were dissatisfied with his actions, but he maintained enough party control to bring about the election of James Madison, who was Jefferson's own choice to succeed him.

Despite the opposition to Jefferson, he had proven himself

Army. The provisions were inspected by a crew of workmen under the direction of two brothers, Ebenezer and Sam Wilson, who represented the army. Sam Wilson, a tall, lean, bearded man, was widely and affectionately known as "Uncle Sam."

A visitor to the supply depot—perhaps a newspaper reporter—saw a workman marking boxes with the initials "E.A.-U.S.," which stood for "Elbert Anderson—United States."

"What do those initials mean?" the visitor asked.

The workman grinned and said, "I don't rightly know, mister—I guess they mean Elbert Anderson and Uncle Sam."

The joke spread and soon cartoons began to appear depicting the United States as a tall, lean, bearded man whose top hat and clothing were decorated with the Stars and Stripes.

In the first half of the nineteenth century "Uncle Sam" wore many different hats. There were those worn by the plain people, those of the rich and greedy, and those of the biased and bigoted, and they were all mirrored in the looking-glass of national politics.

National politics were quite one-sided after the War of 1812. With the Federalist party close to extinction, the Democratic-Republicans were virtually unopposed.

James Madison, who had once bitterly fought against a strong national government, now asked Congress for a bigger army and navy, a standard national currency, an increased tariff to protect American manufacturers from foreign competition, and a great new transportation system of roads and waterways. Congress granted these requests, including establishment of a second Bank of the United States, and the country went on a prosperity spree. Pioneers pushed westward and borrowed money on easy credit to buy farm lands. Land speculators grew rich. New factories mushroomed through the eastern states and inched into the Northwest.

The Presidential election of 1816 came in the midst of the boom. Madison wanted James Monroe, his Secretary of State, to succeed him. Monroe was nominated, and since there was only token opposition from the fading Federalists, his election was assured. After his inauguration in 1817 Monroe visited bustling New England, where a Boston newspaper acclaimed him as the herald of an "Era of Good Feeling."

Another kind of herald appeared in the United States in 1818 in the person of Frances Wright, a twenty-three-year-old Scottish girl who made speeches urging American women to fight for the right to vote and for the abolition of slavery. Some women listened, but most seemed resigned to the tradition that government was entirely man's business, and Miss Wright returned to Scotland aware that her plea was as unheeded as a sneeze in the halls of Congress. However, from time to time, others appeared on the political scene and eventually made their voices heard.

Congress was increasingly concerned with a touch of bad feeling that soon crept into the "Era of Good Feeling." Too many goods and too much borrowing bred a financial panic in 1819, and in the midst of the panic came a political issue that threatened to split the Union in two. The issue was slavery.

In 1819 the Territory of Missouri applied for admission to the Union. Congressman James Tallmadge of New York proposed that slavery be prohibited in the new state and that any slave child, if born after the state was admitted, should be set free at the age of twenty-five. His amendment was defeated.

Slavery had been under fire as early as 1688, but now the

to be a wise, strong and realistic statesman and a great political organizer and leader. Unfortunately these characteristics were not as highly developed in James Madison, his successor.

Madison faced troubles on both land and sea. Americans were pushing westward, slaughtering wild game, slashing the forests, building towns, driving the Indians from their lands and homes. In Indiana Territory an Indian chief named Tecumseh proposed to assemble a confederation of tribes to fight for their rights, and he set up his headquarters on the Tippecanoe River where it flowed into the Wabash. The village was called "Prophet's Town," named for Tecumseh's medicine-man brother, "The Prophet."

In 1810 Tecumseh and a small army of his braves went to Vincennes, the territorial capital, where the chief warned Governor William Henry Harrison that the Indian was through running and would hereafter fight for his home and freedom.

By 1811 the situation was growing worse. Tecumseh notified Harrison that he was leaving for the South to recruit the Creeks. In Tecumseh's absence Harrison led an armed force of 800 men to destroy Prophet's Town. Nearing the village he was approached by a few Indians who pleaded for a pow-wow the following day, and Harrison agreed.

Suspecting treachery, Harrison that night ordered his men to sleep fully clothed and with their guns close at hand. Just before dawn on November 7, 1811, the Indians swooped down on the encampment. Harrison and his men fought a bloody battle for some two hours, until the attackers retreated. The soldiers invaded Prophet's Town, found it deserted, and burned all of its buildings and the surrounding cornfields, then returned to Vincennes. By this action Harrison was proclaimed a hero and credited with making the entire Indiana frontier secure for white settlers.

Harrison and a lot of other people knew that Tecumseh was friendly to the British, and believed firmly that the Indians were being supplied with guns and ammunition by British traders and officials in Canada. This, coupled with British seizures of American ships, raised anti-English feeling to a high pitch in the United States.

A group of young congressional leaders, including John C. Calhoun of South Carolina and Henry Clay of Kentucky, fanned the war spark by denouncing the British and urging the capture and annexation of Canada. These firebrands were given the dubious title of "War Hawks" by John Randolph of Virginia, who opposed their warmongering.

President Madison, convinced by the War Hawks that war with Britain was a necessity, asked Congress on June 1, 1812, for a declaration of war. Although there was vigorous opposition from New England manufacturers, from the Federalist party, and from a great many of Madison's own Republican followers, Congress voted to clash with the British. The War of 1812 was on.

The war lasted for two years. The Americans did not capture Canada, but they did burn two houses of Parliament in Toronto. Later the British invaded the city of Washington and retaliated by burning some of its government buildings, including The President's House, which became known as the White House, after it was painted white to cover the scars of the fire.

On Christmas Eve, 1814, the British and Americans signed a treaty of peace at Ghent, Belgium. Neither side emerged as a conqueror, and the War of 1812 is probably best described as a draw.

On January 8, 1815, knowing nothing about the peace treaty, General Andrew ("Old Hickory") Jackson inflicted a stinging defeat on a British army at New Orleans. More than 2000 British soldiers were killed or wounded, compared to 13 for the Americans.

A new word came into politics at this time and is still in use. The word is *gerrymander*, and one dictionary defines it this way: "Arrangement of the political divisions of a state, county, etc., made to give one political party an unfair advantage in elections."

When Elbridge Gerry was Governor of Massachusetts in 1812 the state legislature enacted a law changing the boundaries of senatorial districts in that state. Before the changes were made, Essex County districts were laid out in such a manner that the Federalists were in the majority. The Democratic-Republicans established new lines so that their own supporters were in the majority.

To do this they had to make so many curves that the outline of the new districts resembled that of a salamander. Benjamin Russell, a Federalist newspaper editor, had a map in his office showing the new boundaries. An artist friend who saw the map penciled in legs, claws, head and eyes and said, "There you are—a salamander!"

"You mean Gerrymander," the editor answered. Although Governor Gerry had not championed the redistricting bill, he did sign it as governor and his name became associated with it and with the salamander.

CHAPTER

4

COMPROMISE, CALHOUN AND "OLD HICKORY"

December 10, 1819: The country is in a bad way, sure enough. When President Monroe was inaugurated two years ago, everything was booming. Folks said we were in an "era of good feeling" and everybody was happy. Today those same folks have been hit by a financial panic—and to make things worse, we're fighting among ourselves about slavery in the new state of Missouri.

November 2, 1827: We have a new political organization—the Anti-Masonic party. It opposes Masons and Masonry on the grounds that Masonic ceremonies are held in secret because they are evil. Stuff and nonsense!

April 4, 1829: Andy Jackson has been in office a month, and already he is throwing government workers out of jobs so he can replace them with members of his Democratic-Republican party. This name is being changed to "Democratic party," but there's nothing democratic about Jackson's spoils system. "Old Hickory" is going to have his hands full with the tariff question and Vice President John Calhoun.

SOON after the outbreak of the War of 1812 the United States was nicknamed "Uncle Sam," supposedly because of a set of initials, a joke and an elderly inspector of army supplies named Samuel Wilson.

A New York contractor, Elbert Anderson, bought a quantity of provisions in Troy, New York, for the United States

COMPROMISE, CALHOUN AND "OLD HICKORY"

United States was expanding, Eli Whitney's cotton gin had made cotton-growing big business, and tobacco also meant riches. Slave labor was both cheap and important to the southern planters. The Territory of Missouri was part of the Louisiana Purchase. If other states carved from that vast land were to be admitted as "free" (non-slave) states, the planters feared that the anti-slavery forces would dominate the Congress and seriously weaken the political strength of the South.

In President Monroe's administration, Congress voted to admit both Missouri and Maine to the Union, which kept North and South in the Senate at equal strength. This legislation was an amendment to the "Missouri Compromise," which provided that slavery would be forbidden in the Louisiana Purchase area north of Missouri's southern border, *except* within the state of Missouri. This satisfied the southerners, but only postponed a violent showdown on the whole slavery question.

A new feeling of nationalism troubled Monroe. More and more people favored a program of internal improvements—roads, canals and other public works—all at the expense of the national government. Monroe, a "strict constructionist" of the Constitution, believed that such matters were the responsibilities of the states, but in this thinking he was opposed even by younger members of his own Democratic-Republican party.

Politically the differences between the industrial North and the agricultural South—differences which had brought earlier clashes between Hamilton and Jefferson—were now magnified and more clearly defined. "Sectionalism" was a growing political problem.

In Monroe's administration Florida was acquired from Spain, progress was made with England in defining northern boundaries of the nation, and a "hands-off" warning was issued to the world. The warning, later known as "The Monroe Doctrine," gave notice that America was henceforth not to be considered a field "for future colonization by any European powers." In part the warning was aimed at Russia, which was threatening to extend its frontiers beyond Alaska and into the Oregon Territory.

Although the Federalist party was practically dead, leaving the Jeffersonian Republicans in power, certain groups developed new ideas and began to form factions under the sectional leadership of such Republican politicians as Andrew Jackson, John Quincy Adams, William H. Crawford and Henry Clay. These four men sought the Presidency in the election of 1824, but when none of the four received a majority of electoral votes it became necessary for the House of Representatives to make the choice.

The House was to choose from the three who had received the greatest number of electoral votes (Jackson, Adams, Crawford). Since Henry Clay was fourth on the list, his name was not considered. Clay was the Speaker of the House and wielded enough influence to throw several votes to any of the three candidates. He used this influence to support John Quincy Adams, who won the election.

When Adams then appointed Clay as his Secretary of State, enemies of the two men promptly set up cries of "Bargain and sale!" or "Bargain and corruption!" and charged that Adams and Clay had made a deal to assure Adams' election. The charge was unfounded, but Clay was unjustly nicknamed "The President-maker."

Clay himself denied the accusation. In one speech to his former constituents he said, "Suppose it were true, as you all know it is not—but supposing it were true that in my long, eventful public career I made a mistake. What then? Supposing your old trusty musket should once misfire, what would you do? Throw it away?"

"No!" someone shouted.

"We'd peck the flint and try her again!" another cried.

Clay had a lot of nicknames in addition to "Presidentmaker." They included "The War Hawk," "The Great Compromiser," and "The Mill Boy of the Slashes." The "Slashes" were the southern swamps around Clay's birthplace in Hanover County, Virginia, and there is a story that Clay cured himself of stuttering by making speeches to cows grazing in the marshes, an exercise which also helped to account for the eloquence that made him famous. He was a bold and brilliant statesman, a great political leader, and an ardent patriot. Friends once warned him that certain statements he proposed to include in a speech against the annexation of Texas might antagonize both political parties and seriously hurt any chance he might have to become President.

Said Clay, "I had rather be right than be President."

At about this time President Adams and his Democratic-Republicans, having seen the last of the Federalist party as an organization, faced a new political force rising up under dramatic circumstances.

George Washington and other Presidents had been members of Masonic lodges, and no one looked upon the fraternal order of Freemasonry as a public enemy until the mysterious disappearance of William Morgan in upper New York State in 1826.

William Morgan, born in Culpeper County, Virginia, had fought with Andrew Jackson in the Battle of New Orleans, and later made his home in Batavia, New York. Word leaked out that Morgan, a disgruntled Royal Arch Mason, was writing a book that would wreck the Masonic Order and expose its rituals and secret aims. Immediately a campaign of persecution was launched against Morgan, apparently by fellow Masons. He was sued by several and jailed repeatedly for nonpayment of debts, some of which were for only two or three dollars.

In September, 1826, Morgan was arrested as a thief and taken to Canandaigua, New York, where he was freed of the theft charge and promptly picked up on another debt complaint and jailed for one day. He was released in the dark of night and was either lured or forced into a carriage and taken to Fort Niagara at the head of the Niagara River. After his abduction Morgan was never seen in town again, and it is probable that he was murdered.

Some time later a body that washed ashore on Lake Ontario, several miles from Fort Niagara, was believed to be that of Morgan, but an investigation indicated that the dead man was one Timothy Monroe. If the body *was* that of Monroe, Morgan's body was never found.

When the story of Morgan's disappearance became known, most people assumed that he had been killed because of his threats to expose the Masons, and this gave them reason to believe that Masonry must indeed be evil. When the first installment of Morgan's book, *Illustrations of Masonry by One of the Fraternity Who Has Devoted Thirty Years to the Subject*, appeared in Batavia in 1826 it triggered the feeling of hatred toward Masonry. Several suspects were arrested for Morgan's abduction and some pleaded guilty to that charge, but there was not enough evidence to convict any of them for murder.

The public boycotted merchants who were Masons, broke off personal friendships and business associations with others.

Even college fraternities such as Phi Beta Kappa suffered because of their secret initiation ceremonies. *All* secret societies were condemned. Scores of Protestant ministers who were Masons were forbidden to preach, and others who were not members of the Order attacked it from their pulpits. The anti-Masonry feeling spread to other northern states and many Masons were fired from public office on the grounds that they could not take secret vows in their lodges and also live up to their oaths of public office. In desperation, thousands of Masons in New York State deserted their lodges and renounced their Masonic oaths.

The climax came in 1827 when the non-Masons in New York founded the "Anti-Masonic" party. In reality the Republican party was the only other organized political group in existence at this time, but it had its own dissenters who also opposed the anti-Masonic objectives. Accordingly, the Anti-Masonic party was considered the first so-called third party on the American political horizon.

The very fact that such a party was organized and widely supported was again proof that our democracy was growing stronger. In many other countries such political opposition would have been swiftly suppressed by the regime in power.

The Anti-Masonic party was not of as much concern to President Adams as was a conflict within his own party. Leader of the opposition was General Andrew Jackson, frontiersman, lawyer, and hero of the Battle of New Orleans in the War of 1812. A victim of tuberculosis and plagued by chronic stomach disorders, Jackson was nevertheless a dynamic and energetic political figure.

Although Jackson, Clay and Adams were all Jeffersonian Democratic–Republicans, the election of Adams divided the party into two camps. One group called themselves "Clay–

Adams men," and their opponents were known as "Jackson men." Soon, however, the Clay-Adams faction took the name of "National Republicans" and the Jackson supporters changed their party designation from "Democratic-Republicans" to "Democrats," a name which has stuck.

With a Presidential election in the offing, the Democrats introduced a bill in Congress which would increase the tariff on such goods as wool, iron, glass, and other raw materials. The higher tariff would protect New England manufacturers, Pennsylvania mine owners, and midwestern sheep raisers against foreign competition, but it would hurt northern shipping firms and the southern cotton planters.

Behind the proposed law was a carefully planned political maneuver. The Democrats introduced the bill as a favor to industry, but purposely set tariff rates extremely high, believing that the manufacturers and shippers would join the southerners to defeat the bill. At the same time, the Democrats in the West could favor its passage, and although they would lose the fight they would be considered as friends of the industrial East. Also, the Democrats of the South would be identified as allies of the cotton-growers.

The scheme fizzled when the manufacturers approved the bill, high rates and all, and the "tariff of abominations" was enacted into law.

John C. Calhoun, Monroe's fiery Vice President from South Carolina, had done his best to keep the bill from passing. Once it was on the books he battled even harder to destroy it. He wrote an "Exposition and Protest," declaring that the tariff was unconstitutional because Congress could impose a tariff only to raise needed money and *not* to "protect" the interests of American manufacturers and others.

Calhoun's document went much further. He argued that since each state in the Union had been called upon to ratify or disapprove the Constitution and its amendments, it should be possible for each state to use the same machinery to judge whether or not Congress had exceeded its powers in enacting new laws. If the state decided that Congress had abused its authority, then the state should declare the objectionable laws null and void within the limits of that state. This was the "doctrine of nullification," and it was adopted by the South Carolina legislature.

The doctrine of nullification could not be really effective unless it was sanctioned or pushed by several other states. To that end, Senator Robert Y. Hayne of South Carolina made a glowing speech about the many advantages the western states would have if they supported Calhoun's argument.

In a debate with Hayne that lasted almost two weeks, Senator Daniel Webster of Massachusetts opposed the doctrine of nullification in some of the greatest speeches in Senate history. Webster argued that if any act of Congress were considered to be unconstitutional, then the question should be decided by the federal courts, and that if each state had the power to nullify laws passed by Congress the result would soon be the breakup of the Union.

Climaxing his appeal to all Americans, Webster pleaded that the Stars and Stripes symbolize not "Liberty first and Union afterwards; but everywhere, spread all over in characters of living light, blazing on all its ample folds as they float over the sea and over the land, and in every wind under the whole heavens, that other sentiment, dear to every true American heart—Liberty *and* Union, now and forever, one and inseparable!"

The question, however, was not yet settled.

The Democrats, with their smooth political machine, rolled up an election victory for Andrew Jackson in 1828 and looked forward gleefully to routing the "aristocrats" from government jobs. John C. Calhoun was re-elected as Vice President.

As Inauguration Day approached, President John Quincy Adams invited Jackson to come to the White House for an informal social visit that was considered customary. Jackson declined, perhaps because he blamed Adams for cheating him of the Presidency in the 1824 election. Because of this rebuff, President Adams packed his bags and belongings and moved out of the Executive Mansion on March 3, 1829, the day before Jackson was to be sworn in.

On Inauguration Day, Jackson walked from his hotel to the Capitol for the ceremony, and when it was over he rode down muddy Pennsylvania Avenue in a carriage followed by one of the largest and most disorderly crowds in the city's history. It was a mob, rather than a crowd, and upon reaching the White House thousands of shouting people fought to elbow and claw their way into the building, tracking mud across floors and rugs, even on chairs and sofas, on which they stood. Gallons of punch were gulped from glasses and pails, and punch bowls and dishes were upset and went crashing to the floor. Some of the merrymakers jumped out of the first-floor windows, apparently all in fun. Jackson himself, disgusted with the whole business, climbed out a window and went to his hotel.

At the time of Jackson's election there were three American political parties—the National Republicans, the Democrats and the Anti-Masons.

This election established geographical divisions between the National Republicans and the Democrats. Jackson was a southerner, Adams a northerner. Sectional differences between

North and South play very important parts in our national political drama.

The aims of the National Republicans were similar to those of the old Federalists. They believed in a strong central government, a national banking system, a tariff that would protect manufacturers and a government-financed program of road-building and other internal improvements. This was the "aristocratic" philosophy of the Hamilton era.

The Democrats, led by Andy Jackson, were for the "plain people," states' rights, against a national bank and a high tariff.

The Anti-Masons professed to be opposed to Masonry and all other secret societies, and stood for the protective tariff and internal improvements at government expense. Andrew Jackson was a high officer in the Masonic Order, and this fact helped to strengthen the Anti-Masonic opposition to him in the 1828 election.

When "Old Hickory" took office in 1829 as the first President nominated by the newly named Democrats, he threw scores of government workers out of jobs, regardless of their ability, and replaced them with people who had served the Democratic cause and were known to be loyal to Jackson himself. Many of his appointees were also expected to "donate" some share of their pay to help carry on the work of the party. This was Jackson's "spoils system," based on the principle that "To the victor belong the spoils of the enemy." It offered a way to repay political favors, either by giving government jobs or awarding work contracts to faithful supporters, many of whom were not capable of doing the jobs properly.

Although this practice was later described in other terms such as "patronage" or "favoritism" (or in some cases "graft"), the spoils system has endured to a great degree in both national and local politics, whatever party is in power.

Vice President Calhoun vigorously opposed the spoils system, thus creating considerable friction between himself and the President. This breach was made wider by Calhoun's doctrine of nullification. On April 13, 1830, birthday of Thomas Jefferson, a big Democratic banquet was held in Washington, attended by President Jackson, Vice President Calhoun, various members of Congress and many prominent citizens.

Up to this time Jackson had not made clear his own views about nullification, and Calhoun believed the President was on his side. When toasts were drunk after dinner Jackson rose from his chair, held his glass high and said loudly and sternly, "The Federal Union—it must and shall be preserved!"

In these nine words the President left no doubt that he was definitely opposed to Calhoun's doctrine.

Then Calhoun stood up to deliver his toast. "The Union," he said, "next to our liberty the most dear; may we all remember that it can only be preserved by respecting the rights of the states and distributing equally the benefit and burden of the Union!"

Jackson's choice of Cabinet officers was undistinguished. Except for Secretary of State Martin Van Buren and Secretary of War John H. Eaton, the members were simply friends of Jackson or Calhoun and were strictly figureheads. For advice and guidance Jackson surrounded himself with a small group of shrewd newspapermen and politicians known as the "Kitchen Cabinet." The term was coined by John Randolph of Virginia, who indicated that these advisers entered the White House secretly through the kitchen door and proposed solutions to the nation's important problems while the real

Cabinet slept. Led by Amos Kendall of Kentucky, who later became Postmaster General, Jackson's Kitchen Cabinet was the first Presidential brain trust.

Throughout Jackson's first term he and his leaders concentrated on building up a strong national Democratic party, and when Jackson ran for a second term the political machine was so efficient that his re-election was practically guaranteed. The Anti-Masons, however, decided that they were now strong enough to nominate a candidate of their own to oppose Old Hickory.

To the Anti-Masonic party goes the credit for holding the first national political nominating convention. Held at Baltimore, Maryland, in September, 1831, the convention nominated William Wirt of Bladensburg, Maryland, as its Presidential candidate.

Wirt was a lawyer who had served as Attorney General of the United States from 1817 to 1829. After he was notified of his nomination he made a dramatic speech to the delegates in which he proudly proclaimed that he was a Mason and defended the Masonic Order! Under the circumstances, he said, the Anti-Masons might want to choose another candidate. The delegates voted unanimously to put Wirt in the race, which indicates that the supposed opposition to Masons and Masonry must have been a minor factor in the party's aim to capture the Presidency.

Three months later, in December, 1831, the National Republicans also held a convention in Baltimore and laid plans for a meeting of its members in Washington in May, 1832. At that time those chosen for this meeting drew up a "party platform"; it was the first time a national political party defined its objectives in writing for the consideration of the voters. The party's Presidential candidate was Henry Clay.

Andrew Jackson and his powerful Democratic party defeated both Clay and Wirt, and he prepared to begin his second term as President. Martin Van Buren was elected Vice President.

On November 24, 1832, only a few days after the election, Calhoun's doctrine of nullification again popped up, this time with a vengeance. A state convention in South Carolina adopted an "Ordinance of Nullification" to fight the protective tariff. Under the ordinance no state or federal authorities within South Carolina could enforce payments of duties imposed by the tariff laws. The ordinance was to become effective on February 1, 1833. Its supporters defiantly declared that if the national government made any move to interfere with South Carolina's commerce, the state would "organize a separate government and do all other acts and things which sovereign and independent states may of right do." In other words, South Carolina would secede from the Union.

After receiving a copy of the ordinance, President Jackson issued a proclamation appealing to the people of South Carolina to "remain in the path which alone can conduct you to safety, prosperity and honor."

The South Carolina legislature authorized the governor to call out the state militia to enforce the ordinance and to buy ammunition and other military supplies.

John C. Calhoun resigned as Vice President on December 28, 1832 (his term was to expire March 3, 1833) and became a senator from South Carolina, feeling that in the Senate he could wield greater influence in gaining support for his doctrine. Thus the nation was without a Vice President until Martin Van Buren took office March 4, 1833. As a senator, Calhoun took an oath to support the Constitution of the United States.

An irate President Jackson sent troops, a warship and several revenue cutters to Fort Moultrie in Charleston Harbor, prepared to enforce the federal tariff laws. Although this show of force cooled the rebellious attitudes of many people, it angered others. One day a delegation of Jackson supporters from South Carolina called on the President.

"Our lives aren't safe," they reported. "The nullifiers claim that all Union men better leave South Carolina if they don't want to be sent out in coffins!"

The President picked up his corncob pipe from the desk, rubbed the bowl with his thumb, then pointed the stem at his visitors. "You go back to Charleston," he said softly, "and tell the nullifiers that if a hair on the head of a Union man is harmed, that moment I order General Coffee to march on Carolina with fifty thousand Tennessee volunteers." Now his voice boomed. "And if that doesn't settle the business, tell 'em—by the Eternal!—that I'll take the field myself, with fifty thousand more!"

On February 12, 1833, Senator Henry Clay introduced a compromise tariff bill which eliminated tariffs on certain goods and proposed a gradual reduction of others over a ten-year period. The bill was passed, South Carolina did not offer forcible resistance to the tariff, and the very real threat of secession faded away for the time being.

During Jackson's second term a miracle saved him from death. On January 30, 1835, the President attended a funeral at the Capitol. After the services, as he left the rotunda to go to the east portico, a small well-dressed young man with a pale face, black hair and dark eyes, stepped in front of Jackson, yanked a pistol from under his coat and aimed point-blank at the President at a distance of about six feet. The hammer fell, but the gun failed to fire.

Instantly the man whipped out another pistol and pulled the trigger, but again the shot did not go off.

Startled by the quick attack, Jackson leaped at the assassin. Friends near the President tried to hold him and seize the attacker, but Jackson cried, "Let me alone! Let me alone! I'm not afraid. I can take care of myself!"

Several men hauled the would-be killer away, and later the police tested both of the pistols by firing several shots from each gun. Every shot fired perfectly! The chances of two misfires in succession, such as those aimed at Jackson, were estimated by experts to be one in a hundred thousand.

The attacker, Richard Lawrence, thirty-five years old, blamed the President for personal financial troubles. The jury found him guilty by reason of insanity and he was committed to a hospital for the insane.

In Jackson's second administration the Democrats referred to the National Republicans contemptuously as "Whigs." Just as "Democrats" grew from a term of derision, the National Republicans adopted the nickname and now became the "Whig" party, which gradually absorbed the Anti-Masonic party.

During the Revolution the term "Whig" was synonymous with "patriot," and it is probable that the party leaders hoped that the revival of the name would have a favorable psychological effect in attracting voters. In addition, however, the party picked up strength from many Anti-Masons and from Democrats whom Jackson had antagonized by throwing them out of government jobs or by failing to reward them for their political services.

Jackson created dissension in his own party by his veto of a bill to renew the national banking system and by substituting state-chartered banks for a central bank. Charters were often issued by corrupt officials, many officers of state banks stole depositors' funds, others speculated and lost, and bank failures became common. A group of Democrats in New York County broke away from the national party and formed what they called the "Equal Rights" party, dedicated to revising the banking system and to fighting monopolies.

In 1835 the members of this Equal Rights party attended a noisy gathering in Tammany Hall, New York City, headquarters of the Tammany Society which had supported Jackson in his struggle against a national banking system. The meeting had been called by the "regular" Democratic party to confirm the nomination of one Gideon Lee as a candidate for Congress. Lee was strongly opposed by the Equal Rights party, and when the call came for a chairman for the meeting the gas-lighted hall became as noisy as a roomful of hog-callers in rehearsal. The Equal Rights supporters shouted in favor of their chairman, while the Democrats screamed "Shut up!" and yelled for order.

Suddenly the gaslights dimmed and died, plunging the hall into darkness. Apparently some "regular" Democrat guarding the gas line figured that the Equal Rights party would give up and leave, but he was quite mistaken. First at one end of the room, then at the other, and then here and there in between, like fireflies, tiny flames popped up as the Equal Rights men struck "locofoco" or "self-lighting" matches. They brought out candles which they lit and held up, for they had anticipated this very emergency.

Reluctantly the "regular" Democrats marched out of Tammany and to Military Hall, where they spent the evening denouncing their opponents.

When the story of the ruckus appeared in the New York *Courier and Enquirer*, the newspaper referred to the Equal Rights group as the "Locofocos." The happy Whigs seized upon the term and applied it to the Democratic party as a whole, which for a long time was called the "Locofoco" party in various sections of the nation.

Despite its name-callers, the Democratic party under Jackson's leadership was solidly in control of the government. The Whigs were principally people of wealth and property who disliked Jackson because he fought monopolies, was against a national banking system, favored the farmers and working classes, and supported a reasonably low tariff as a means of revenue rather than a high tariff that would protect the northern manufacturers against foreign competition.

In the Presidential campaign of 1836, Jackson told his party leaders that he wanted Martin Van Buren nominated as his successor. Some of the leaders were reluctant to support Van Buren but were afraid of Jackson, and the Whig opposition quickly declared that "King Andrew the First" was proposing to crown a new monarch of his choice and set up a dynasty that would perpetuate the Jacksonian principles.

Instead of nominating a single candidate to oppose Van Buren, the Whigs nominated four different men in the hope that all four would poll so many electoral votes that Van Buren would lose and it would become necessary for the House of Representatives to choose the President-elect. In that event, political pressures could influence the votes of certain congressmen. The strategy failed, and although the popular vote was close, the election was a victory for both Van Buren and Jackson.

"Old Hickory" left the Presidency as one of America's

truly great political leaders and a rugged symbol of government by the people. The Democratic party, which he had helped weld into a smooth and powerful machine, was a living monument to his genius as an organizer and his respect for the strength of "the common man."

CHAPTER

5

TIPPECANOE AND BIGOTS, TOO

October 5, 1840: The Whigs are really whooping things up for their Presidential candidate, "Old Tip" Harrison. Their "hard cider and log cabin" campaign is completely new to the voters, who are having so much fun they don't give a hoot about party platforms. There hasn't been much fun since Martin Van Buren took office in 1837, mostly because of widespread unemployment, inflation, land speculation and crop failures. If "Old Tip" wins the election, things can't get much worse and may get better.

July 6, 1844: Bigotry is on the march. The Protestants are afraid the Roman Catholics want to take over the country for the Pope, so the Protestants are ready to burn them out, beat them up and send them packing. This month there were anti-Catholic riots in Philadelphia, and the whole unpleasant situation is getting out of hand.

August 9, 1848: Today a new political baby was born—the Free Soil party. A little earlier there were two others—the Barnburners and the Hunkers—and we've also had the American Republican party and the Liberty party. Only in a democratic system such as ours could one find so many organized groups openly seeking control of the government by a vote of the people.

MARTIN VAN BUREN was born on a farm in Kinderhook, New York, in 1782, six years after the Declaration of Independence was signed, which means that he was the first President of the United States who was not born a British subject.

Davy Crockett said that when Van was one year old "he

could laugh on one side of his face and cry on the other at one and the same time." In his long career in public service Van Buren showed himself to be a shrewd and brilliant politician, master of so many tricks that John Quincy Adams nicknamed him "The Little Magician" and others called him "The Red Fox." He would need all of his foxy magic to get the country out of the muddle that began soon after he took office in 1837.

In Andrew Jackson's administration the building of roads and canals and the expansion of the western frontier had led to wildcat speculation in lands and securities. Instead of levying taxes to raise money for making internal improvements, many states had borrowed from their state banks. Scores of these banks later collapsed, including several in which the federal government had deposited large sums. Depositors became paupers over night. Farm crops failed, and farmers who owed money were unable to pay their debts. Factories closed and thousands of men were unemployed. A boom in counterfeiting helped to deteriorate the currency and spread the panic. Nobody wanted to buy goods and everybody wanted to sell.

These were some of the principal reasons why the United States plunged into a major economic depression in 1837, and although many of the reasons had grown from the policies of Andrew Jackson, Van Buren's administration was blamed for the disaster.

Times were still bad when election time came in 1840. Once again the Democrats nominated Van Buren. Their Whig opponents' candidate was General William Henry Harrison, with John Tyler for the Vice Presidency.

Now a new political party entered the race, with James G. Birney of New York as its nominee. This group called itself the "Liberty" party, and its major objective was the abolition of slavery, a distasteful subject which thus appeared in a national political campaign for the first time.

Formation of the Liberty party was due in part to the crusading of William Lloyd Garrison of Massachusetts who, even while in his teens, was writing forceful anonymous newspaper articles about the evils of slavery. When he was only twenty-six Garrison and a partner, Isaac Knapp, published a newspaper, *The Liberator,* whose editorial policies were opposed to slavery, liquor, tobacco, capital punishment and Freemasonry. In its first issue on January 1, 1831, Garrison wrote: "I am in earnest—I will not equivocate—I will not excuse—I will not retreat a single inch—and I will be heard!"

Garrison and Knapp had little money and no subscribers, and although the paper gradually picked up business, the two men were so poor that they slept on the floor in their printing shop.

Garrison's strong views won him both friends and enemies. The state of Georgia, claiming that his crusade was so inflammatory that it violated Georgia's laws, offered a reward of $5000 for his arrest and conviction. The newspaper office was flooded with letters branding him a troublemaker, some even threatening to kill him.

The Liberator became a growing and powerful anti-slavery influence, and Garrison seized every chance to make speeches in favor of abolition. One of his proposals was to separate the free from the slave states, dividing the country. During one appearance in Boston he was hauled from the speaker's platform by his enemies, who hung a rope around his neck and dragged him through the city streets until police came to his rescue and took him into protective custody.

Garrison's paper and speeches helped to foster the Liberty

party, and he and his abolitionist followers (including such people as James Greenleaf Whittier, Henry Wadsworth Longfellow and Wendell Phillips) organized the "Underground Railroad" in Massachusetts, a movement designed to assist runaway slaves to escape to Canada.

In the Harrison–Van Buren campaign of 1840 the Democrats favored Van Buren's financial policy of an independent treasury and his program of internal improvements. They did their best to overlook the devastating financial panic which had plagued the country under Van Buren's leadership, although the voters would not soon forget it.

The Whigs, on the other hand, had no platform at all! Instead, they introduced a famous "first" to politics—a razzle-dazzle campaign of ballyhoo and showmanship that was entirely new to the voters and which set the pace for lively campaigns in the election years ahead.

In part, the new campaign was due to some nasty remarks printed in the Baltimore (Md.) *Republican*, whose editorial policy favored the Democrats. The newspaper article ridiculing Harrison said that if he were to receive "a pension of $2000 and a barrel of cider, General Harrison would no doubt consent to withdraw his pretensions and spend his days in a log cabin on the banks of the Ohio."

This shot at "Old Tip" Harrison backfired when some Whig ancestor of a modern Madison Avenue advertising genius conceived the idea of using barrels of cider, log cabins and coonskin caps as symbols of William Henry Harrison, "plain man of the people."

As a reminder of his victory over the Indians at Tippecanoe, Harrison's backers created a catchy slogan for his political campaign: "Tippecanoe and Tyler too!"

The Democrats, seeking a battle-cry of their own, came up

with "Crow, Chapman, Crow!" Joseph Chapman, a Democrat of Greenfield, Indiana, was a small-town political prophet, and his one prediction in every Presidential campaign was that the Democrats would win in *every* county in Indiana.

The Whigs made jokes about Chapman's "crowing," and soon Chapman and crowing were synonymous. As in past name-calling contests, the Democrats decided to turn this one to their advantage. They created a picture symbol of a rooster and a crow to represent the Democratic party, and it was widely used in newspapers and campaign literature.

Harrison's promoters had only begun. They built a number of log cabins, mounted them on wheels, put barrels of hard cider in the open doorways, hung axes, rifles, deerskins and coonskins on the walls, and filled each cabin with Whig whooper-uppers, who drank some of the cider and ladled some out to prospective voters as the log cabins rolled through town after town.

This was the kind of political campaign that is found today only in the history books. In one area the log cabin parade was two miles long! As it approached each town it was heralded by several brass bands riding in gilded wagons drawn by magnificent white horses, with trumpets and trombones blaring "Hail, Columbia!" and "The Star-Spangled Banner." Whigs on foot flanked the parade, and both the walkers and riders carried signs with such inscriptions as: OLD TIP— THE PEOPLE'S FRIEND. OLD TIP NEVER LOST A BATTLE FOR YOU. VOTE FOR THE LOG CABIN AND HARD CIDER CANDIDATE.

If the parade arrived in a town at night, thousands of lighted candles flickered in windows, on the roofs and in the hands of happy people on the streets. Men, women and children danced around huge bonfires, sending weird shadows galloping across building fronts. In one town the fires and people were drenched by a sudden heavy downpour, and the next morning the streets were seas of mud in which horses sank almost to their bellies, yet the townsfolk turned out to help the parade on its way with shouts of "Hurray for Tippecanoe and Tyler too!"

One Pennsylvania group of twelve men rolled a ten-foot-high rubber ball through the streets. The ball was covered with slogans and the men sang verses such as "With Tip and Tyler we'll burst Van's b'iler!" They also shouted, "Let's keep the ball rolling!"—a cry that became part of our language.

There was no point in discussing political "issues" in this new kind of campaign, which is exactly what the Whigs wanted. The people were having fun and the Whigs were gaining the votes they set out to get.

Moaned the Democrats, "We've been sung down, lied down and drunk down!"

The Democrats tried in all sorts of ways to discredit Harrison. In one political meeting in Columbus, Ohio, a politician named William Allen sneeringly declared that after the War of 1812 General Harrison was presented with a woman's petticoat as a symbol of, and reward for, his military prowess. The Whigs branded Allen a "liar and a scoundrel" and one challenged him to a duel that never came off. The Democrats claimed that Allen's story could be proven by a Mrs. Crissand, who had allegedly quilted the petticoat.

Although Mrs. Crissand was then on her deathbed, the Whigs sought her out and obtained her sworn affidavit that she had never quilted any such petticoat. When the affidavit was made public, William Allen was promptly christened

"Petticoat" Allen, a nickname which stuck to him for the rest of his career.

Thanks to the whoop-de-do, the ballyhoo and the hard cider, Harrison won the close election. Unfortunately he died in April, 1841, after only one month in office, and John Tyler became President—the first Vice President in our history to succeed to the highest office.

By reason of this first succession, was John Tyler the President or merely "Acting" President? To resolve any doubts he appeared before Justice William Cranch of the Circuit Court of Appeals and asked Cranch to administer the oath of office as taken by the President. After the oath was sworn, Tyler had Judge Cranch certify in writing that although Tyler "deems himself qualified to perform the duties and the powers and office of President . . . without any other oath than that which he has taken as Vice President, yet as doubts may arise and for greater caution . . ." he took the Presidential oath, thereby setting a precedent which has since been followed.

Tyler was a southerner and an aristocrat whose political views were so different from those of the late President Harrison that the Whigs thought him a stanch Democrat, a traitor to their cause. As the time approached for another election Tyler tried unsuccessfully to interest the Democrats in making him their candidate.

One rival for the Presidency was again James G. Birney, nominated by the Liberty party, which renewed its platform against slavery. The other candidates were Henry Clay for the Whigs and James K. Polk for the Democrats.

Originally the two major Democratic prospects were Martin Van Buren and General Lewis Cass, who had been Secretary of War in Andrew Jackson's Cabinet. The southerners didn't want Van Buren and the northerners objected to Cass, so the party looked for a compromise candidate and found James K. Polk, who became not only the nominee but also the first "dark horse" in American politics.

A political "dark horse," in other words, is a candidate who is nominated (usually unexpectedly) when a convention cannot agree on one of the principal contenders.

Although Polk was elected, it is probable that he would have been defeated by Henry Clay except for two things. One was that Birney, the Liberty party candidate, polled several thousand votes that might otherwise have gone to Clay. The other was that the Democrats unlawfully "naturalized" thousands of Irishmen and other aliens in return for promises that these newly made "citizens" would vote for Polk.

The influx of hundreds of thousands of foreigners was a growing problem that brought about the creation of a new political force founded on bigotry and religious intolerance. The first breath of this party was drawn in 1843 when a group called the "Native American Association" was organized in New York with the avowed intention of keeping Roman Catholic and Irish immigrants (most of whom *were* Roman Catholics) from becoming American citizens or from holding local or national government jobs.

Roman Catholicism as an alleged danger to the country was stressed by the "Protestant Reformation Society" in the late 1830s, but it was brought sharply into focus about 1842 in New York City when a group of Catholics objected to public school teachers who read to their classes from the King James (Protestant) version of the Holy Bible. Protestant propagandists distorted the real facts to make it appear that the Catholics were against *any* reading from *any* Bible.

Adding more fat to the fire was the fact that a financial depression still existed and that many newly arrived Irishmen, working for low wages, had deprived native-born Americans of their jobs.

The "nativism" propaganda induced scores of Protestant ministers to attack the Pope and the Roman Catholic Church from their pulpits, and thousands of gullible Protestant families were transformed into rabid Catholic-haters.

Leaders of the Protestant Reformation Society, seizing their opportunity, formed the "American Republican" party in 1843, with a platform that was anti-Catholic and anti-alien.

The hate campaign was bound to bring violence, and it did. In Philadelphia in May, and again in July, 1844, mobs of Protestants, fired up by rabble-rousers, stormed through the city streets with clubs and torches, yelling, "Down with the Pope!" "Get the Catholics!" and "Burn 'em out—burn 'em down!"

In a frenzy of hate they smashed their way into homes where foreigners were known to live, thrashing those families who failed to flee, pillaging as they went, and setting fire to scores of houses. Catholic schools went up in flames, and the rioters put the torch to the building occupied by the Hermits of St. Augustine (now St. Augustine's Roman Catholic Church).

Called to quell the riots, the state militia set up cannon in the streets as troops waded into the battle. Some semblance of order was restored after both sides suffered losses. One account says that two soldiers and seven civilians were killed. Another claims that there were more than twenty dead and almost a hundred wounded. The only satisfying result was that thousands of people who formerly sympathized with the

American Republican party were shamed and disheartened by the riots, and cut themselves loose from all association with the organization. The Protestant Reformation Society and the American Republican party went into eclipse—but they were soon to shine again under other names.

In 1846, in the midst of this turmoil, President Polk asked Congress for two million dollars to buy certain Mexican territory, and a bill was introduced accordingly. To this bill Congressman David Wilmot of Pennsylvania proposed an amendment reading:

> Provided, That, as an express and fundamental condition to the acquisition of any territory from the Republic of Mexico by the United States, by virtue of any treaty which may be negotiated between them, and to the use by the Executive of the moneys herein appropriated, neither slavery nor involuntary servitude shall ever exist in any part of said territory, except for crime, whereof the party shall first be duly convicted.

Known as "the Wilmot Proviso," this amendment was defeated, but it served to set the policy of those who opposed the extension of slavery. In brief, they would not fight to have slavery abolished in states where it was already in effect, but they would combat all attempts to introduce it in new territory.

New territory was about to be acquired.

The Republic of Texas, which had gained its independence from Mexico in 1836, was admitted as a state of the Union in 1845. There was no clear definition of the western boundary of the state, and a vast expanse of land stretched from Texas to the west coast. To the south, the United States claimed that the Rio Grande River marked the Mexican border, while the Mexicans insisted that the more northern Nueces River was the international boundary line. To back up the American claim, President Polk sent troops commanded by General Zachary Taylor into the disputed Rio Grande zone as an army of occupation.

The Mexicans rushed in an army of their own to challenge this invasion of what they considered their land. On April 24, 1847, an American military patrol was attacked by the Mexicans, and on May 13 Congress formally declared war on Mexico.

One Whig congressman from Illinois argued that there was some doubt as to whether or not General Taylor's patrol had been attacked on land which rightfully belonged to the United States, and believed that the resulting war was unnecessary and unconstitutional. The congressman's name was Abraham Lincoln.

The war ended February 2, 1848, with victory for the United States. By the Treaty of Guadaloupe Hidalgo, Mexico gave Upper California, Utah, Arizona and New Mexico to the United States and agreed that the Rio Grande marked the southern boundary of Texas. As part of the treaty the United States paid Mexico 15 million dollars.

Immediately this newly acquired land became a political issue. The South saw a chance to expand slavery, and the North opposed any such expansion.

When the 1848 election campaigns were launched the strongest Whig candidate was Henry Clay, whose pro-slavery sentiments were well known. Clay wanted the Whig party to disclaim any desire to acquire territory for spreading slavery. The southerners, called "Cotton Whigs," were therefore opposed to him, and the northerners, known as "Conscience Whigs," were against him because of his previous defenses of

Inauguration of George Washington as the first President of the United States (From a painting by Clyde O. DeLand)

Thomas Jefferson,
Father of the
Democratic Party

President John Adams
(From a painting by
John F. Copley)

President Andrew (Old Hickory) Jackson

James Madison's ideas and proposals formed the basis for the Constitution of the United States

For a long time the rooster was the symbol of the Democratic Party

Political sheet music helped campaigners to sing the praises of Whig candidate Harrison in the 1840 "hard cider" campaign (Photo by H. E. Neal)

Lucretia Mott was an ardent crusader for women's rights

Harriet Beecher Stowe's *Uncle Tom's Cabin* helped to point up the evils of slavery

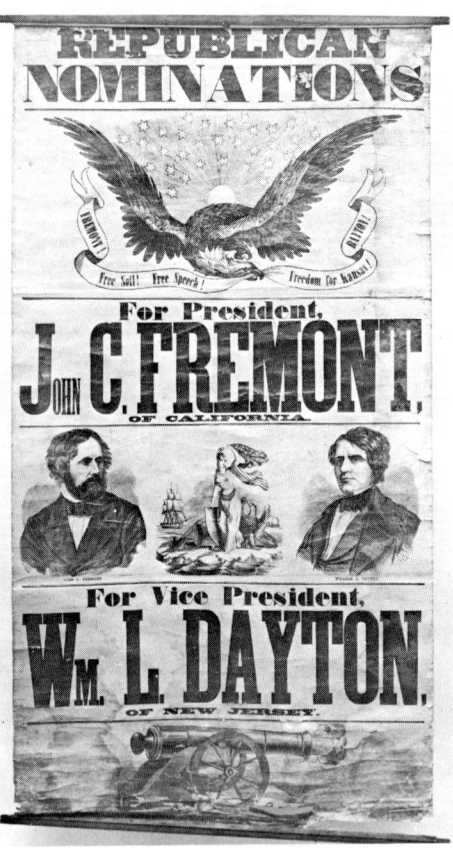

1856 "Free Soil" Fremont-Dayton banner (from the Ralph E. Becker Collection of Political Americana)

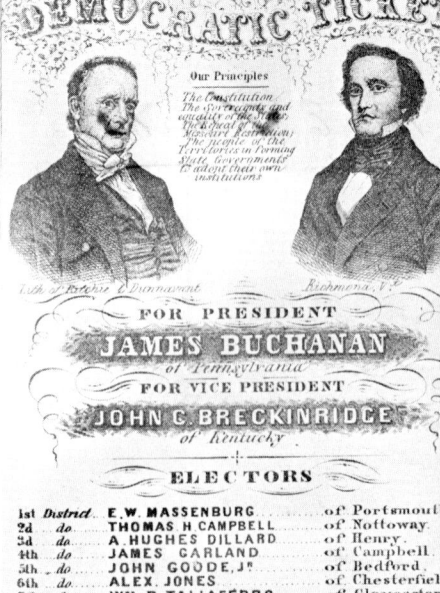

1856 ballot (from the Ralph E. Becker Collection of Political Americana)

Political "singing commercials" were popular long before the radio-TV era (from the Ralph E. Becker Collection of Political Americana)

1860 Lincoln-Hamlin campaign ribbon (from the Ralph E. Becker Collection of Political Americana)

Abraham Lincoln in the field during the Civil War, with Allan Pinkerton (l.) and General J. A. McClernand

The donkey as a symbol of the Democratic Party made his debut in this Thomas Nast cartoon

Elizabeth Cady Stanton (L.) and Susan Brownell Anthony pioneered in the fight for woman suffrage

Belva A. Lockwood, one of the first women candidates for the Presidency, ran in 1884 and 1888 on The Equal Rights Party ballot (from the Ralph E. Becker Collection of Political Americana)

ELECTORAL TICKET
—OF—
THE EQUAL RIGHTS PARTY
State of Kentucky,
1888.

FOR PRESIDENT,
BELVA A. LOCKWOOD,
Washington, D. C.

FOR VICE PRESIDENT,
ALFRED H. LOVE,
Philadelphia, Pa.

DISTRICT ELECTORS:

1—WM. R. BUSH, - - - - Smithland.
2—D. G. SEBRIE, - - - Hopkinsville.
3—WM. T. COX, - - - Bowling Green.
4—CHAS. JOVLYNE, - - Hardin County.
5—JOHN HOYLAND, - - - Louisville.
6—HENRY QUEEN, - - - - Newport.
7—HOWARD GRATZ, - - - Lexington.
8—MRS. JAMES BENNETT, - Richmond.
9—SAMUEL PEACEMAN, - Rowan County.
10—MRS. ELIZABETH REID, Mt. Sterling.
11—GENERAL GRIFFIN, - - Somerset.

ELECTORS AT LARGE.

J. G. CRADDOCK, - - - - - - Paris.
J. E. BOSLEY, - - - - - Winchester.

The elephant as a symbol of the Republican Party was first used in this cartoon by Thomas Nast, published in *Harper's Weekly,* November 7, 1874

It was from a N cartoon like this t fugitive "Boss" Twe was identified in Sp and returned to t United States and j (*Harper's Weekly* c toon from the Ralph Becker Collection Political Americana

William Jennings Bryan's "Cross of Gold" speech made him famous but failed to win him the Presidency

dent William McKinley, e election was largely o the support and activi- f Mark Hanna

Theodore Roosevelt headed the "Bull Moose" Party in 1912 and lost to Woodrow Wilson

Picture made by George W. Harris to contradict rumor that Wilson was too ill to continue as Chief Executive. Mrs. Wilson held an official document which the President's paralyzed arm was unable to steady

Copyright by Harris & Ewing

Campaign button (From the Ralph E. Becker Collection of Political Americana)

1928 Herbert Hoover and Al Smith Toby mugs (From the Ralph E. Becker Collection of Political Americana)

Al Smith listens as FDR sings about recovery and the New Deal (Cartoon by Berryman in the *Washington Star*)

President Franklin D. Roosevelt signing the formal declaration of war against Japan. Standing (L. to R.): Sen. Alben Barkley, Sen. Carter Glass, Rep. Joseph Martin, Sen. Tom Connally

Dwight D. Eisenhower, President of the United States, 1953–1960

John F. Kennedy, President of the United States, 1961–1963

Lyndon B. Johnson, President of the United States, 1963–1969

Richard M. Nixon, President of the United States, 1969–

slavery. For these reasons the party decided that Clay could not get enough support to win the nomination or the election.

The Mexican War had just ended, Zachary Taylor's victories were fresh in all minds, and he was acclaimed as a military hero. He was a southerner who owned some three hundred slaves, and he would be sure to get votes, even in the North. But was he a Whig? Nobody knew. Taylor had never voted, and his political leanings were his own secret. After considerable urging and argument Taylor announced that he was a Whig, but warned that if he were elected he would run the government his way and would not stand for any dictation from the party. With this understanding he was nominated by the Whigs, who chose Millard Fillmore of New York as their Vice Presidential candidate.

The Democrats were having their internal troubles, too. One faction that was more interested in sharing the spoils of an election than in the slavery fight was called the "Hunkers," a name said to be based on the Dutch *hunk*, or *honk*, meaning "post." The "post," in a children's game, was similar to a base in baseball, and a player who was "hunkered" (on base) was safe. In the political sense the Hunkers were conservatives. A different version is that the name was applied to those who "hunkered" for soft government jobs.

Another group, the "Barnburners," was dead set against slavery and in favor of paying off the states' debts with money that the Hunkers wanted to spend to build canals. The name "Barnburners" grew from a story about a Dutch farmer who was so plagued by rats in his barn that he burned the barn to the ground to get rid of the pests.

At the Democratic convention in Baltimore the rivalry between these two factions resulted in a walkout by the Barnburners and a refusal to vote by the Hunkers. The convention finally settled on Lewis Cass as the party's candidate, but avoided an out-and-out stand for or against slavery.

The disgruntled Barnburners opposed Cass and held their own convention in Utica, New York, where they nominated Martin Van Buren for the Presidency.

Now a brand new party was in the making. The Barnburners had nominated Van Buren. At a convention in Buffalo, New York, on August 9, 1848, the New England "Conscience Whigs," the Barnburners, and some members of the Liberty party combined to support Van Buren as President and Charles Francis Adams as his running mate. Their major platform plank was strong opposition to slavery in any new territory.

As part of its platform this group said, "We inscribe upon our banner 'Free Soil, Free Speech, Free Labor and Free Men!' " Because of this slogan this combination of political forces became known as the "Free Soil" party.

In the 1848 elections Zachary Taylor won the Presidency, mostly because the Democratic vote was split between Cass, the Democrat, and Van Buren, the Free Soiler.

One of the first American conventions of its kind was also held in 1848 in the Wesleyan Methodist Church in Seneca Falls, New York. It was a convention for women's rights, led by Mrs. Elizabeth Cady Stanton and Miss Lucretia Mott, two abolitionists who pioneered in a battle to give American women the right to vote. The convention did not produce any world-shaking developments, but it did help to attract more women to the cause.

Among these was Mrs. Amelia Jenks Bloomer of Homer, New York, who startled the country in 1849 by appearing publicly in an unusual costume which she urged other women to wear in the interests of health and comfort. The costume consisted of a tight-sleeved short jacket, a skirt whose hemline was just below the knees, and a pair of very loose and flowing trousers such as those worn in Turkey, held tightly around the ankles by elastic bands. Although the "bloomers" were not a rousing success, several women did wear them, including Elizabeth Stanton.

While the women were just starting to mobilize, the religious fanatics were again on the march. The Protestant Reformation Society gave way to the "American Protestant Society," bent on the "salvation" of all Roman Catholics. It was supported by most Protestant churches and ministers, and once again the preachers derided the Pope from their pulpits. Two other Protestant groups, the Foreign Evangelical Society and the Christian Alliance, had similar aims, but they were much smaller than the American Protestant Society, and in 1849 the latter absorbed both of them. From this merger came "The American and Foreign Christian Union," whose ambitious purpose was to "purify" Christianity, not only in America but also in Europe or "wherever a corrupted Christianity exists."

Not all Protestants in America were fanatics, of course. The propagandists built up the fear that the Pope intended to conquer the United States by sending Roman Catholics into the country in great numbers, later to rise up and take over. The fact that nearly half a million immigrants, mostly Catholics, were arriving in America every year helped to convince many Protestants that the stories were true and that some action had to be taken to protect themselves and their religious liberty. Sermons and pamphlets were not enough. They must take a hand in the government itself.

The anti-Catholic sentiment had brought about the formation of several large and small organizations, some secret, some open. One of the most active secret groups was "The Order of the Star-Spangled Banner," set up in 1849 in New York City, complete with secret handshakes, secret passwords and secret ceremonies. Seeking strength through unity, this order merged with several others, including "The Order of the Sons of America," the American Protestant Society, and the United American Mechanics; and in 1850 this combine formed the "Native American" party, an anti-Catholic political force fed by bigotry and intolerance.

Although the very name of this party symbolized its objective, its plans were not publicized and its members were sworn to secrecy. If a "Native American" were asked outright about his party's organization or workings, or even about his own political objectives, he had a stock three-word answer: "I know nothing!"

One newspaper cartoon of the day showed a man, suitcase in hand, at a New York pier asking two other men how to find the "Know Nothing Lodge." One answers, "If you have any valuables in your bag, you'd better not take it into the lodge, because if you can't find it when you're coming out, nobody will know nothing about it!"

The party's propaganda included songs composed especially to keep the hate fires burning. Here's a sample from a ditty about Papal Bulls (which were orders or announcements issued by the Pope):

> 'Tis said the darned Know Nothing tickets
> Have given the Roman Church the rickets.
> One thing we know, the Roman bull
> Americans can never rule.

> Out of the way, you're quite too late,
> You bullhead beast of the Papal State!

Horace Greeley, New York newspaper editor, is generally credited with naming the Native American party the "Know Nothing" party, a nickname which stuck through its rather brief but influential life.

CHAPTER

6

REPUBLICANS AND REBELLION

January 1, 1851: Prospects for a Happy New Year are not bright. The Compromise of 1850 added more fire to the slavery question, which is growing more serious every day. As if that isn't bad enough, Elizabeth Stanton and that pantaloon Bloomer woman are continuing their agitation to give women the right to vote. Next they'll want to smoke and drink!

July 6, 1854: Senator Steve Douglas is boasting that he alone pushed through the Kansas-Nebraska bill to permit new states to decide whether they shall be slave or free. As a result of this law we now have a new political party made up of a coalition of Whigs, Democrats and Free Soilers. Its members call themselves "Republicans."

April 12, 1861: It is reported that the secessionists are bombarding Fort Sumter in Charleston Harbor. If the report is true, then we are at war with ourselves. This crisis will test the mettle of President Lincoln; may God guide his hand.

TENSION was increasing over the slavery question. In legislation known as the Compromise of 1850 Congress admitted California as a free state, thus making the North more powerful than the South in the Senate; abolished slavery in the District of Columbia; and enacted a Fugitive Slave Law which helped the South by authorizing United States marshals to arrest runaway slaves and penalized anyone who helped such an escaped fugitive. The compromise set up the new territories of Utah and New Mexico, carved from former Mexican holdings. When admitted as states, should these new territories have slavery or not? The compromise provided that they could be admitted "with or without slavery, as their constitution may prescribe at the time of their admission." This was the principle known as "popular" or "squatter" sovereignty.

The compromise widened the breach between the northern Whigs and the southern Whigs and marked the beginning of the breakup of the Whig party.

Feelings for or against slavery had grown stronger year by year. In Cincinnati, Ohio, in 1833 a feud broke out between the people of the city and the faculty and students at the Lane (Presbyterian) Theological Seminary. The townspeople accused the school of "fomenting trouble" by spreading abolitionist propaganda; the school was indeed vigorously opposed to slavery. Relations finally became so strained that the seminary's director, the Reverend Lyman Beecher, ordered both students and professors to halt all abolitionist activity.

In protest, a number of students quit the seminary, along with some teachers, including Professor Theodore Weld, and went to Oberlin, Ohio, an abolitionist stronghold, where they later founded Oberlin Collegiate Institute (now Oberlin College), the first "integrated" and first coeducational college in the United States. From this institution Weld and his followers fanned out over the country, making speeches and distributing literature to gain support for the abolitionist cause.

A copy of one of Professor Weld's pamphlets fell into the hands of Mrs. Harriet Beecher Stowe, whose husband, Calvin, was a professor at Lane Seminary. Based upon the facts in the pamphlet, coupled with her first-hand observations of and talks with slaves at work in Kentucky, Mrs. Stowe wrote a book, *Uncle Tom's Cabin, or Life Among the Lowly*, in which she made a strong indictment of slavery. It was first published in installments in the *National Era*, an abolitionist paper in Washington, D. C., and in 1852 came out in book form in Boston. Mrs. Stowe was worried that no one was reading her work.

Her worries were groundless, for the sales of the book totaled half a million copies within five years after its publication. It helped to crystallize the North's anti-slavery sentiments, and it was one more grain of powder added to a bomb that was bound to explode.

Mrs. Stowe's book gave great satisfaction to Elizabeth Stanton, Lucretia Mott and Amelia Bloomer, who were now firmly in the fight for abolition and women's rights. In 1851 Amelia Bloomer brought a new ally into the ranks, a schoolteacher named Susan Brownell Anthony. She was aggressive, domineering and energetic, and despite her deep spiritual feelings she was known to use strong language whenever she was aroused by critics and hecklers. Miss Mott and Mrs. Stanton believed that she was the dynamic force needed to put the woman suffrage movement into high gear.

While the ladies laid plans to get their program rolling, other more urgent plans were in progress in Washington, where Democratic Senator Stephen A. Douglas of Illinois spearheaded a drive in 1854 to get congressional enactment of the "Kansas–Nebraska bill." Under this proposed law the Nebraska Territory would be split into two territories, one to be called Kansas, the other Nebraska. Both were in the area defined in the Missouri Compromise of 1820, which prohibited slavery in the Louisiana Purchase land except in Missouri itself. Now, however, Senator Douglas and his allies proposed to kill the Missouri Compromise.

The Kansas–Nebraska bill would repeal the Missouri Compromise and permit Kansas and Nebraska (or any other territories), when admitted as states, to decide for themselves whether or not they wanted slavery.

This bill tore the major political parties into splinters. Democrats and Whigs alike had factions for and against the bill and for and against slavery in general. The slavery Whigs, not choosing to unite with the slavery Democrats, joined the Know Nothing party, which changed its official name from the Native American to the American party, and with this patriotic title picked up considerable strength. Many of its own members, however, bolted the party to join the anti-slavery Whigs, Democrats and Free Soilers in an "anti-Nebraska" movement, believing that their best course was to organize a brand new party with the unified aim of fighting the slavery forces.

The first recorded steps toward forming such a party were taken in the Congregational Church in Ripon, Wisconsin, on February 28, 1854, when Major Alvan E. Bovay, a prominent Whig, called a meeting of Whigs, Free Soilers and Democrats. The meeting adopted a resolution providing that if the Kansas-Nebraska bill passed, the existing Ripon party organization should be abandoned and that a new Republican party should be formed.

Under Senator Douglas' leadership the bill did pass the Senate in March, and on March 20, 1854, Major Bovay called a second meeting in Ripon, which voted to dissolve the local Whig and Free Soil parties and to form a new Republican party.

This action was a splendid example of the fact that practically every American political party, large or small, has helped to make stronger our democratic system of government. In this case, for instance, Whigs, Free Soilers and Democrats formed a new alliance, the Republican party, which was simply another "splinter" party supported by dissatisfied followers of other political faiths—but it was to become one of the most influential and progressive forces in American political history.

There is some disagreement as to whether the Republican party was christened in Ripon or in Jackson, Michigan. According to the Republican National Committee, the formation of the new party and the use of the name "Republican" had been discussed by Major Bovay as early as 1852 with Horace Greeley, editor of the New York *Tribune*. The Committee also quotes Major Bovay as saying, "We went into the little [Ripon] meeting as Whigs, Free Soilers and Democrats. We came out of it Republicans, and we were the first Republicans in the Union."

By prodding and promising and arguing and browbeating, Senator Douglas won his victory, for after a bitter debate lasting several days and nights the Kansas–Nebraska Bill passed the House of Representatives on May 22, 1854, by a vote of 113 to 110.

On July 6, 1854, a formal convention met in Jackson, Michigan, and adopted a resolution that included this statement:

> RESOLVED, That in view of the necessity of battling for the first principles of Republican government, and against the schemes of an aristocracy, the most revolting and oppressive with which the earth was ever cursed or man debased, we will cooperate and be known as 'Republicans' until the contest be terminated.

Joseph Warren, editor of the Detroit *Tribune*, credited himself, Jacob M. Howard, chairman of the Resolutions Committee, and Horace Greeley with the choosing of the name "Republican" (and according to a congressional document published in 1946, "The name 'Republican' was formally adopted by a state convention at Jackson, Mich., on July 6, 1854").

When the Kansas-Nebraska Bill became law, Senator Douglas boasted, "I passed the Kansas-Nebraska Act myself! I had the authority and power of a dictator throughout the whole controversy in both Houses."

On July 4, 1854, even as the new Republican party planned its anti-slavery program, the abolitionists staged a huge Independence Day celebration at Framingham, Massachusetts. The principal speaker was William Lloyd Garrison, who savagely attacked the Constitution of the United States because, he said, it permitted slavery under the law instead of making it a crime.

"The Constitution," Garrison shouted, "is a covenant with death and an agreement with Hell!"

To climax his attack he set fire to a copy of the Constitution.

As for the pro-slavery South, many slave-owners were rushing to set a precedent by putting their slaves to work in Kansas. Northerners also swarmed into the new territory, determined that it should never become a slave state. The result was a bloody civil war in Kansas that lasted for a year or more.

The Kansas trouble also caused the brutal beating of a United States senator in the Senate chamber itself.

In a shocking two-day speech called "The Crime Against Kansas," Senator Charles Sumner of Massachusetts had ripped into earlier pro-slavery remarks made by Senator Andrew P. Butler of South Carolina. After the Senate adjourned on May 22, 1856, Senator Sumner sat alone at his desk in the quiet chamber, writing, when he heard his name spoken by a man standing at his side. He looked up and saw a thirty-seven-year-old giant, Congressman Preston S. Brooks of South Carolina, who held a stout cane in his hands.

Brooks said, "Mr. Sumner, I have read your speech carefully and with as much calmness as I could be expected to read such a speech. You have libeled my state and slandered my relative, Senator Butler, who is old and absent, and I feel it my duty to punish you for it!"

Without further warning Brooks lifted the heavy cane and brought it down on Sumner's head. Although stunned by the terrific blow, Sumner instinctively tried to stand up to defend himself. His legs, hitting the bottom of his desk, tore it loose from the floor to which it had been fastened with screws. With blood streaming down his cheeks he attempted to ward off more strokes with his arms, but Brooks, with his Herculean strength, pounded the senator's head and shoulders unmercifully, even when Sumner slumped moaning to the floor, virtually unconscious. The cane broke after the first vicious onslaughts, but Brooks kept up the savage attack until he was seized by two senators from New York who rushed into the chamber upon hearing the commotion.

After an investigation by the House of Representatives, a resolution to expel Brooks was defeated and Congress voted merely to "censure" him. In a fiery speech about this rebuke Brooks said, "If I desired to kill the senator from Massachusetts, why did I not do it? You will all admit I had it in my power.... Ten days ago, foreseeing what the action of the House would be, my resignation was put into the hands of the governor of South Carolina. And now, Mr. Speaker, I announce to you and to the House that I am no longer a member of the Thirty-fourth Congress!"

When he returned to South Carolina, Brooks was wined

and dined as the idol of the hour, and when an election was held to fill the vacancy created by his resignation he was elected unanimously and returned to Congress. A few months later Brooks was stricken with a throat infection and died by strangulation.

The Republican party was at first organized in only a few states, but began to recruit new members rather quickly. Like the original Federalists, the Republicans stood for a national bank currency, for protective tariffs and internal improvements. Their major attraction, however, was the assertion that the federal government had power to control slavery in the territories.

The first national convention of the Republican party was held June 17, 1856, in Philadelphia, and nominated John C. Frémont of California for the Presidency. A convention speaker, Henry S. Wilson, declared that the party's principles were "free speech, a free press, free soil, free Kansas—" and was interrupted by a voice in the crowd yelling, "And Freemont!"

The year 1856, marking the birth of the Republican party in convention, also marked the death of the Know Nothing party as a political power. After the exodus of those who went over to the Republicans, the ones who remained were divided on the slavery issue. The party's 1856 candidate, Millard Fillmore, received only the electoral votes of the state of Maryland, and the Know Nothings finally Had Nothing.

The election was won by the Democratic candidate, James Buchanan, a mild and elderly man from Pennsylvania, who had the powerful backing of Tammany Hall. He had a double chin and a habit of carrying his head cocked to one side, as though suffering from a stiff neck or, like a puppy, listening to some new and strange sound. He considered slavery to be "merely a difference of opinion, a matter of little practical importance," but only two days after he took office the Supreme Court handed down a decision that made the slavery agitation worse than ever. The decision involved a slave named Dred Scott, who had brought suit in a federal court to gain his freedom on the grounds that he had traveled with his master into "free" territory.

Briefly, the Supreme Court decision said that Scott was a Negro slave, that no Negroes of slave descent were American citizens, and that Scott therefore had no right to sue in a federal court. In addition, said the Court, the Missouri Compromise was unconstitutional. A slave was merely "property," and Congress had no right to keep "property" out of any territory.

This famous decision delighted the slaveholders and enraged the anti-slavery forces. Instead of settling the issue it merely complicated it.

The new Republican party attracted more and more members. One Whig who became a Republican was an Illinois lawyer named Abraham Lincoln. Lincoln had served in the state legislature and also served one term as a United States congressman from Illinois, so that he was widely known in that state, and in 1858 the Republicans decided to enter him as their candidate for the United States Senate.

In accepting the nomination Lincoln said, "A house divided against itself cannot stand. I believe this government cannot endure permanently half slave and half free. I do not expect the Union to be dissolved, I do not expect the house to fall, but I do expect it will cease to be divided. It will become all one thing or all the other. . . ."

Lincoln's Democratic opponent was Senator Stephen A. Douglas of Kansas–Nebraska fame.

Douglas was one of the finest orators of his day, yet Lincoln challenged him to public debates about the current political issues, the foremost being the slavery question. In the seven debates that followed, great crowds assembled to see and hear these two politicians. In appearance they were in striking contrast. Douglas was short, rather handsome, carefully groomed and tastefully dressed. Lincoln was tall, rawboned and homely, wearing tight-fitting clothes that were well-wrinkled and made him seem gawky and graceless.

A friend in talking with Lincoln made fun of Douglas' short legs.

Lincoln squelched him with a smile, saying, "I always thought a man's legs should be just long enough to reach the ground."

On one occasion Senator Douglas said that he remembered Lincoln as a mere "grocery keeper" who sold cigars and whiskey.

Answered Lincoln, "What Mr. Douglas has said is true enough. I did keep a grocery and I did sell cotton, candles, cigars and sometimes whiskey. Many a time have I stood on one side of the counter and sold whiskey to Mr. Douglas on the other side, but the difference between us now is that I have left my side of the counter, and Mr. Douglas still sticks to his as tenaciously as ever!"

The debates covered the principle of "squatter sovereignty," the Kansas–Nebraska Act, and the Dred Scott decision. Douglas, the orator, the spellbinder, defended "squatter sovereignty" and the Dred Scott decision. He also made interpretations of some of Lincoln's remarks which Lincoln claimed were distorted.

"I am not a master of language," Lincoln said. "I have not a fine education. I am not capable of entering into a disquisition upon dialectics, as I believe you call it; but I do not believe that the language I employed bears any such construction as Judge Douglas puts upon it. . . ."

Lincoln then forced Douglas to concede that he didn't care whether slavery was "voted up or voted down," and to say that he believed a United States territory could "exclude slavery from its limits prior to the formation of a state constitution." The South was opposed to Douglas' stand, and the Democratic party was thus split wide open.

Although the campaign closed with a victory for Senator Douglas, it served to center national attention on Abraham Lincoln, and in 1860 he became the Republican candidate for the Presidency, with Hannibal Hamlin as his running mate.

The Democrats, meeting in April in Charleston, South Carolina, could not agree on a platform. One group wanted a strong stand in favor of the southern planters and slavery in the territories, and another insisted upon a more moderate approach that would help to get northern support. The moderates won, but the whole party lost, because the delegates from nine states walked out in protest.

One of the Democratic factions held a separate convention and nominated Senator Douglas as its Presidential candidate. The other chose John C. Breckinridge of Kentucky, a slaveowner and ardent supporter of the slavery interests.

Now a new political party appeared. Made up of conservative Democrats, old-line Whigs and former Know Nothings, the "Constitutional Union" party opened its convention in Baltimore, Maryland, on May 7. Its members, believing that the country was nearing the brink of a civil war, had no platform as such, but declared that "it is both the part of patriotism and of duty to recognize no political principle other than the Constitution of the country, the Union of the states, and the enforcement of the laws."

Because its candidates were John Bell of Tennessee for President and Edward Everett of Massachusetts for Vice President, many people called it the "Bell and Everett" party. Bell, once a Democrat, later a Whig leader, had been a United States senator and Secretary of War under President Harrison. He was a stanch patriot, devoted to the Union, and although he lost the election he did poll more than half a million popular votes.

The votes for Bell and the breakup of the Democratic party insured a victory for the Republicans, and Abraham Lincoln became President of the United States at one of the most crucial periods in the country's history.

In December, 1860, South Carolina formally seceded from the Union, and early in 1861 other southern states followed. In March a permanent Constitution was drawn for the Confederate States of America, and Jefferson Davis of Mississippi and Alexander H. Stephens of Georgia were elected President and Vice President of the Confederacy.

On April 12, 1861, a Confederate farmer–volunteer fired the first cannon shot in a bombardment of Fort Sumter in Charleston Harbor; and from the fort came an answering roar from a cannon fired by Captain Abner Doubleday, "father of the game of baseball." Thus began a shooting war that was to be one of the bloodiest in history.

A great many northern Democrats supported the President and the Republican party in a common cause—saving the Union. This fusion of "War Democrats" and Republicans, known during the war as the "Union" party, gave the Republicans complete control of Congress.

President Lincoln also won the loyal support of William Lloyd Garrison, the abolitionist, and of Lincoln's former rival, Senator Douglas.

It would be a long time before the Democratic party regained its strength. When the Civil War ended in 1865 there were tremendous problems of reconstruction facing the wounded nation—and all kinds of schemers, connivers, crooks and rogues were on the prowl, in politics and out.

CHAPTER

7

CARPETBAGS, LADIES AND TAMMANY HALL

April 10, 1867: Carpetbaggers and scalawags have plundered the South since Mr. Lincoln was killed two years ago. The Ku Klux Klan and other secret societies that sprang up as defenders have now become terrorists and murderers.

December 10, 1870: That Stanton woman and her radical friends, still fighting for woman suffrage, have been joined by Victoria Woodhull and have formed an association to press for a Constitutional amendment. We have even heard rumors that the Woodhull woman hopes to be a candidate for the Presidency!

June 12, 1874: A lot of farmers who joined Oliver Kelley's Granger movement, seeking relief from the hard times that began last year, are now going whole hog into politics by forming their own "Greenback" party. Also, there is news that a new political organization called the "Social Democratic Workingmen's" party has been started in New York by a bunch of foreigners who want to abolish capitalism.

March 2, 1877: The special Electoral Commission finally decided that Rutherford Hayes beat Sam Tilden for the Presidency by one vote! Tilden's supporters are ready to spill blood to contest the decision.

HORSEWHIPS, lynch ropes, clubs, guns and flaming crosses were used by hooded gangs to "influence" voters and politicians in the period of reconstruction after the defeat of the Confederacy.

These secret "societies" began as a means of self-protection against some acts of a vengeful Congress. President Lincoln died from an assassin's bullet on April 14, 1865, and was succeeded by Vice President Andrew Johnson. Johnson was anxious to help rebuild the South and restore the Union, but was bitterly opposed by certain lawmakers known as "Radical Republicans," led by Congressman Thaddeus Stevens and Senator Charles Sumner.

The Union party of the war era had been made up of Republicans and War Democrats. With the coming of peace the Democrats were returning to their own party and the Republicans sought a way to build up their declining strength. By political pressure and legislation the Radical Republicans in Congress deprived thousands of white southerners of the voting privilege, maintained military rule in the South, and at the same time permitted more than half a million Negroes to vote, organizing them through the Union League of America. As a result the governments of several southern cities and states were run by corrupt white politicians, "scalawags" and "carpetbaggers," with whom many former Negro slaves collaborated.

The term "carpetbagger" was common in the 1830s in the West, when confidence men braved the frontier and opened "wildcat" banks. Some morning a town would awake to find its only bank closed and the banker gone, along with his depositors' money. Usually the crooked "bankers" carried all their possessions in a carpetbag—a kind of suitcase made of carpetlike cloth—which was all they needed when the time came to flee with their loot. The name "carpetbagger" was another term for "thief."

When the war ended, thousands of northerners flocked into the devastated South. Many were sincerely anxious to help the southern states in their recovery, but others wanted only to rob and plunder. The robbers were the carpetbaggers. Those southerners who gave them any assistance were the "scalawags" (slang for scoundrels or riff-raff). Together they schemed to control the local governments and to take over many southern homes and farms.

Angry southerners, seeking a way to fight back, organized two secret societies in 1867. One was the "Knights of the White Camellia" and the other was the "Ku Klux Klan." Here and there smaller secret groups were formed—the Invisible Circle, the Pale Faces, the White League—and gradually the name of the Ku Klux Klan came to be associated with all or most of them.

However peaceful its aims started out to be, the KKK soon became a terrorist organization. Some of its members dressed in long white robes with masks and pointed hoods; others wore the hoods with coats and pants bearing mysterious emblems. They stormed into the homes of Negroes and local public officials, flogging them with horsewhips or beating them with clubs. In many cases the KKK murdered its enemies by shooting or lynching. A congressional investigating committee found that in 1868 there had been 18 murders and 315 floggings in 14 counties of North Carolina, 72 murders and 126 whippings in 29 Georgia counties, and more than 1000 killings in Louisiana.

Symbol of the Klan was a flaming cross, and when the ruthless reputation of the Klan spread across the South its members burned wooden crosses in the front yards of families it wanted to terrorize so that they would be afraid to vote or to take any active part in local government.

President Andrew Johnson's plans for reconstruction paralleled many of those Lincoln had expressed before he was murdered, and Johnson figured that he could put many of these plans into operation before Congress convened and without congressional approval. He was quite mistaken, for the Radical Republicans looked upon him as an enemy. They sought some basis for removing the President from office, but could find none until Johnson himself supplied it.

Johnson had "inherited" Lincoln's Cabinet members, including Secretary of War Edwin M. Stanton. A confirmed Radical, Stanton opposed Johnson at every opportunity, and the President finally suspended him as head of the War Department. Stanton refused to get out and ordered the arrest of Lorenzo Thomas, whom Johnson had appointed as Acting Secretary. As Johnson had hoped, the whole matter was now in the hands of the courts, which would decide whether or not Stanton's dismissal was Constitutional under the "Tenure of Office" Act.

The "Tenure of Office" Act provided that Cabinet members would serve during the term of "the President by whom they may have been appointed and for one month thereafter." Johnson's stand was that Stanton had been appointed by Lincoln and that he, Johnson, had the right to fire him.

The Radical Republicans were not interested in Constitutional law—only in their political necessity of getting rid of President Johnson. They withdrew the charges in the courts and on February 24, 1868, the House of Representatives began impeachment proceedings, charging the President with committing "high crimes and misdemeanors."

A majority of two-thirds was needed for conviction—and since the Republicans had more votes than that, they felt sure they would win. At voting time, however, seven independent Republicans chose to vote against impeachment, and Andrew Johnson retained his office by a single vote!

In 1871 Johnson's successor, President Ulysses S. Grant, ordered the Ku Klux Klan and similar unlawful organizations to disband, and hundreds of Klansmen were arrested. Gradually the southern states enacted "Jim Crow" laws which deprived the Negro of his rights, and the secret societies were dissolved.

The expression "Jim Crow" is said to have originated in Charleston, South Carolina. A hotel owner had two Negro slaves, both named James. So that he could call one or the other and not have both respond, he designated one as "Jim," the other as "James." Because Jim's skin was considerably darker than that of James, many of the hotel guests referred to Jim as "Jim Crow," after the well-known black bird.

Although the carpetbag governments did institute some progressive reforms in education, taxation, transportation and other fields, the southern Democrats were fast regaining control of their state legislatures. As a result of the reign of terror, the passage of "Jim Crow" and other new laws, and a common aim to help themselves, all southern states were bound together in what become known politically as "the Solid South."

Not all northerners were out to pounce upon the vanquished South. Many had a real desire to help in rebuilding. One who translated this desire into action was Oliver Kelley, an employee of the Department of Agriculture in Washington.

In 1866 Kelley had visited a number of southern farms and was amazed to discover that outmoded, slow and clumsy agricultural methods were still in use. Kelley got the idea that he could help farmers to help themselves by holding meetings where they could not only talk about their problems, but also hear experts tell them about modern and improved farming methods. In the North as well as the South, farmers were increasingly concerned about the continued building of new factories, the growth of railroads and mushrooming freight rates, and the steady decline of prices for vegetables, meat and other farm products.

Kelley and a few friends, including one William Saunders, made plans for a new kind of organization, complete with a secret ritual and seven degrees, offering membership to farmers and their families, including children more than fourteen years old. It was called the "Patrons of Husbandry," with a series of local lodges, each known as a "Grange," which in England was a term synonymous with "farm." The first Grange was organized December 4, 1867, in Washington, D. C., with William Saunders as Master.

At first Oliver Kelley seemed unable to get much active support from farmers in organizing other local Granges, but in 1868 he went to his home state of Minnesota and introduced his idea to his farming friends and neighbors. It caught on when the farmers saw in it a chance to fight the high freight rates and to set up their own "cooperatives," where they could both buy and sell farm goods and escape middlemen's profits and manufacturers' monopolies.

The farmers were not the only ones having troubles. Scandals in the Grant administration caused a split in the Republican party. Certain Cabinet members teamed up with crooked businessmen to defraud the government. Other officials "sold" government jobs. New industries were springing up, especially in the North and West, and their wealthy owners spent money freely to influence federal officials and to buy favors from the government. President Grant was thoroughly honest, and although he had proven himself to be a skilled general, he was never a real politician. Those around him simply took advantage of his political innocence and were responsible for the inefficiency and graft that clouded his Radical Republican administration.

Despite the need to clean their own house the Republicans, looking toward the next election, continued to criticize their Democratic rivals at every opportunity. Political figures and issues had for years been praised or condemned in all sorts of newspaper and magazine cartoons, a device that has become practically universal. One of the best-known cartoonists of the Civil War and Reconstruction periods was German-born Thomas Nast, who came to the United States as a child of six and was educated in New York City.

Nast was a Republican reformer who worked for various papers and magazines in the United States and Great Britain, and became a staff cartoonist for *Harper's Weekly*, using his talents to build good will for the Republican party. In *Harper's Weekly* for January 15, 1870, a Nast cartoon was published showing a donkey (representing the Democratic party) kicking a dead lion (representing the deceased Secretary of War Edwin M. Stanton). The caption: "A live Jackass kicking a dead lion. And such a lion! and such a Jackass!" When readers showered Nast and the magazine with praise for his choice of symbols, the artist continued to use the donkey as his image of the Democrats, and the Democratic Donkey became familiar as the party symbol.

Democrats and Republicans alike were being pressured by the supporters of the Stanton–Mott–Anthony woman suffrage team, who had been working steadily toward their goal. They had tried in 1868 to have the word "male" eliminated from the Fourteenth Amendment to the Constitution, which related to citizenship and also to the "right to vote" being "denied to any of the male inhabitants" of the states. The ladies lost.

In 1870 the states ratified the Fifteenth Amendment, which

provided that "The right of citizens of the United States to vote shall not be denied or abridged by the United States or by any state on account of race, color, or previous condition of servitude." In this Amendment the "suffragettes" had fought to have the word "sex" inserted—but they lost again.

Susan Anthony and Elizabeth Stanton were more determined than ever, and in 1870 they formed the National Woman Suffrage Association to sponsor a Sixteenth Amendment for woman suffrage. In the same year Henry Ward Beecher and Lucy Stone (who urged women to retain their maiden names after marriage) organized the American Woman Suffrage Association. Its aim was to work toward amending *state* constitutions, thus giving women the right to vote in various states.

At about this time both Susan Anthony and Elizabeth Stanton teamed up with Mrs. Victoria Woodhull, an ardent believer in woman suffrage, who had made a fortune with the financial help of millionaire Cornelius Vanderbilt. Their alliance with Mrs. Woodhull led to the first serious rift between Miss Anthony and Mrs. Stanton. It came when Mrs. Stanton pledged herself *and* Miss Anthony to change the National Woman Suffrage Association to the "People's" party, headed by Mrs. Woodhull. Mrs. Stanton signed Susan Anthony's name to the pledge without Susan's permission. When Susan heard about it she was so angry that she broke off with Mrs. Woodhull and strained her friendship for Elizabeth Stanton.

The "People's" party later changed its name to the "Equal Rights" party and in 1872 held a convention in Vineland, New Jersey, nominating Victoria Woodhull for the Presidency, and a Negro orator and writer, Frederick August Washington Bailey, for the Vice Presidency. Bailey later became famous under the name of Frederick Douglass as a Negro leader, a public official, a great speaker, and Minister to the Republic of Haiti.

Mrs. Woodhull (called by some "The Terrible Siren") received several thousand votes in the election. Her candidacy apparently convinced certain politicians that there was something to be gained by favoring women's rights, for the National Prohibition party came out in favor of woman suffrage and the National Republicans in 1872 proposed that "respectful consideration" be given to the women's objectives.

In the midst of the suffrage fight and the big party battles, two more new parties made their entrance. Sponsored by the National Labor Union, the "National Labor Reform" party convened at Columbus, Ohio, in 1872 and nominated Judge David Davis of Illinois as its Presidential candidate. This party advocated sharing the wealth, higher pay, shorter working days and better working conditions. Judge Davis later withdrew from the contest and both the union and the party disbanded.

The second new contender was the "Temperance" party, which held its first convention in Columbus in February, 1872, and chose James Black of Pennsylvania as its Presidential candidate, with the Reverend John Russell of Michigan for the Vice Presidency. The party's aim was to enact laws against the manufacture and sale of all intoxicating liquors.

As political corruption continued within the government, many Republicans joined with groups of Democrats to oppose the unscrupulous dealings of Grant's underlings and won such public support that they called a national convention in Cincinnati, Ohio, in May, 1872. Here another new party, the "Liberal Republican" party, was born. It nominated Horace Greeley for the Presidency, B. Gratz Brown, Governor of Missouri, as his running mate, and was supported by a large number of Democrats who called themselves the "Liberal Republican Democratic" party.

Other Democrats who chose to go their own way met in Louisville, Kentucky, in September, as the "Straight-Out Democratic" party and nominated Charles O'Conor of New York and John Quincy Adams. Both men refused to accept the nomination, but the party kept their names in the race anyway and polled some 30,000 votes.

The Radical Republicans again nominated Grant, who was re-elected.

In 1873 the country plunged into a disastrous financial depression and the farmers in several states flocked to join Oliver Kelley's Grange organization in the hope that it could save them from utter ruin.

Although the "Granger Movement" itself was not a political party, it had led hosts of farmers into political activities. Its united members soon became strong enough to organize independent "Anti-Monopoly" parties in several states, and in some cases they teamed up with the Democrats. Besides fighting for lower taxes and government reforms, the Anti-Monopolists demanded that state laws be enacted to regulate big corporations, especially railroads. In a few states the party succeeded in getting legislation restricting the railroads and freight rates so severely that the railroad companies almost went bankrupt. The result was that the stringent laws were repealed or modified, and the farmers gained some relief.

This was not enough, however. When the farmers learned that the Grange was not a cure-all for their financial troubles they organized a new rescuer, the "Independent" party, which soon became known as the "Greenback" party.

"Greenbacks" was the name given to paper money of the United States authorized by an Act of Congress in 1862—

the first federal money issued since the days of the Constitution. The bills were called "greenbacks" because their reverse sides were printed in green. At first they were not backed by gold, and soon after they were issued they began to decline in value, creating inflation, so Congress passed a law to take the greenbacks out of circulation.

The Greenback party opposed this move, demanded that more greenbacks be put into circulation, and that they be used in redeeming government bonds, which were legally payable in gold. Since the principal opponents of the Greenbackers were the Republicans, many Democrats backed up the demands of the Greenbackers purely for party reasons.

The farmers were not the only group trying to climb out of the economic rut into which they were thrown by low prices for farm products, high prices for necessities, and the declining value of money. A European influence was creeping into American politics. In London a German revolutionist named Karl Marx had written books urging "workers of the world" to fight for the common ownership of all products and production, and rule by the proletariat (the laboring class) instead of the bourgeoisie (property owners). Marx's communistic proposals could be summed up in four words: "Abolish all private property!"

In 1864 Marx had helped to organize an "International Workingmen's Association" in London, designed to unite the world's workers to overthrow capitalism. This was known as the "First International," and as its symbol the organization chose a red flag. For this reason the term "Red" was later applied to revolutionists and anarchists.

In 1872 the First International moved its offices from London to New York City, intending to convert Americans to the Marxist goal. Under its leadership a new political group, the "Social Democratic Workingmen's" party, was organized in 1874 by a labor union known as the "United Workers of America," whose members opposed capitalism.

Also in 1874, when the Republican party was weakening, another famous Thomas Nast cartoon gave birth to the elephant as the Republican party emblem. According to the Republican National Committee, here is the story behind the cartoon:

In the spring of 1874, the year after Grant had entered upon his second term, the old New York *Herald* published an editorial representing Grant as a Caesar plotting to overthrow the unwritten law against a third term and to make himself a dictator. Although the charge was untrue, the Democrats picked it up for use as political ammunition. Designed not so much as a serious attack on Grant as it was for a newspaper sensation to increase circulation, what started as a *Herald* publicity stunt succeeded in distorting the political situation and frightening even some Republicans away from the party fold.

At about the same time the *Herald* concocted another story to raise its circulation. This was the famous Central Park Menagerie scare of 1874—a successful hoax. The *Herald* story said that the animals in the zoo had broken loose and were roaming about the wilds of Central Park in search of prey. The whole town was excited until it developed that the story was a fake.

Combining both incidents in the November 7, 1874, issue of *Harper's Weekly* was a Nast cartoon showing an assortment of wild animals fleeing from a donkey wearing a lion's skin labeled "Caesarism." One fleeing animal was an elephant, marked "The Republican Vote." The donkey supposedly represented the New York *Herald* in the lion's skin of "Caesarism."

Says the Republican National Committee, "The symbol of the elephant was used because among its characteristics are cleverness and unwieldiness; easily controlled until aroused, the elephant is yet unmanageable when frightened. Here were all of the characteristics of the Republican vote about to be shown in the coming election—the cry of 'Caesarism' about to panic the Republican vote away from the Republican candidates."

For the caption of his famous cartoon Nast used part of a fable by Aesop: "An ass, having put on the lion's skin, roamed about in the forest and amused himself by frightening all the foolish animals he met within his wanderings." In the full fable Aesop told how the ass betrayed himself by his braying. Aesop's moral was: "Fine clothes may disguise, but silly words will disclose a fool."

In later cartoons the elephant symbolized the Republican party.

In a convention at Indianapolis, Indiana, on May 17, 1876, the Greenback party nominated eighty-five-year-old Peter Cooper of New York and Samuel F. Cary of Ohio as its Presidential and Vice Presidential candidates, and although Cooper polled no electoral votes he did get 80,000 popular votes.

Sometimes referred to as "The Crime of '76," the 1876 election of Republican Rutherford B. Hayes came close to pushing the United States into another civil war. Hayes' Democratic opponent, Samuel J. Tilden of New York, polled thousands more popular votes than Hayes, but ran into trouble in the electoral college. Three southern states—South Carolina, Florida and Louisiana—had "carpetbag" governments whose electoral votes might swing the election to Democrat or Republican. The Republicans sent messengers into these three states to try to bring the electors into the Hayes camp, and were accused in some quarters of having paid large sums of money to seal the bargain.

The confusion was great, mostly because of disputes about the counting and the validity of certain returns. Party protests indicated that the electoral college procedure would result in a deadlock that might extend beyond Inauguration Day, March 4, which would leave the nation without a President. A new law was swiftly enacted (the Electoral Commission Law of 1877) setting up an Electoral Commission to make a final decision on the electoral votes. This commission consisted of five senators, five representatives, and five justices of the Supreme Court. Seven of the men were Democrats, seven were Republicans, and one—Judge Davis—was an independent, but the Democrats believed that Davis was a Tilden supporter and therefore on their side.

During the week in which the Commission was to make its decision Judge Davis became a senator from Illinois and relinquished his judgeship, so he left the Electoral Commission and was replaced by another justice who was a Republican. Thus the Republican members were now in the majority.

On March 2, only two days before inauguration, the Commission announced that Rutherford B. Hayes, the Republican, had received 185 votes to Tilden's 184.

Angry Democrats cried "Fraud!" and came up with a slogan, "Tilden or blood!" They were ready to battle with bullets.

Tilden's friends urged him to fight the Commission's decision, but he declined for at least two reasons. First, he was not in good health; and second, he realized that if he did consent to rally his followers they would not hesitate to take up arms in his behalf and make a battlefield of the nation that was just recovering from the wounds of another war. Thus Rutherford B. Hayes became President of the United States in 1877. He withdrew Union troops from the last of the carpetbag southern states and ended the so-called Reconstruction Period.

During 1877 the Social Democratic Workingmen's party, founded by the United Workers of America, changed its name to the Socialist Labor party, marking the first time the word "Socialist" was used officially in the name of an American political party.

The Hayes administration, in 1878, saw the end of the reign of William Marcy ("Boss") Tweed of Tammany Hall, a politician who made corruption a million-dollar career and a synonym for Tammany.

Until about 1860 Tammany Hall was similar in most respects to other political organizations, but when Tweed became its leader Tammany was transformed into a mighty political machine that could and did make or break many a candidate for public office.

"Boss" Tweed's methods for controlling votes took many forms. He had himself appointed as Street Commissioner and put unscrupulous associates in various important public offices. He made gifts to the poor. To Roman Catholics he professed to hate Protestants, and vice versa. Bribery was merely a useful political device.

As a good example of Tweed's crooked operations, consider the building of a new courthouse. Contractors carefully estimated that the construction would cost about $250,000. The work was begun, but before the building was even completed the city got a bill for $1,149,874.50 for "repair of fixtures."

Another bill for "thermometers" totaled $7500. One carpenter charged $360,747 for his work, but this was nothing compared to $2,870,464 claimed by one plasterer for nine months' labor.

Many of the materials bought for the courthouse were actually delivered to a hotel owned by Tweed's son, but Tweed himself took a huge cut of the tremendous sums paid from the city treasury.

For a considerable time the people of New York were ignorant of Tweed's crooked dealings. Although the politicians knew what was going on, they were too aware of Tammany's power to say anything against the "Boss." One of Tweed's hirelings, however, a man named O'Brien, who was a small-time party worker and errand-runner, thought he should get better pay for his services. He had a friend list all the payments made in the courthouse deal and used this list to try to blackmail "Pete" Sweeney, the City Treasurer, into paying him "hush money." When Sweeney kicked him out of his office, O'Brien gave his list to *The New York Times*.

The *Times* exposed Tweed and his gigantic swindle. Tweed sent a messenger to offer the newspaper owner five million dollars to kill any other stories and to take a vacation abroad. The newsman refused. Based on the *Times* revelations a citizens' committee made a thorough probe of Tweed and his dealings, with the result that Tweed and some of his accomplices were arrested for fraud.

Tweed was sentenced in November, 1873, to twelve years in jail, but after he served a year the sentence was reduced to one year. The moment he was released he was arrested again and held under three million dollars bail until he repaid at least six million dollars he had stolen from the city. Unable to raise the bail, Tweed was imprisoned once more, but even in jail he had such influence that he was allowed to visit his home under police guard. During one such visit on December 4, 1875, he left the police officers sitting in his parlor while he scooted out the back door, disguised himself as a sailor, and made his way to Spain.

In Spain he was identified from a Thomas Nast cartoon and was returned to the United States. He died in jail April 12, 1878, but many techniques of his "boss rule" in politics set a pattern which would live for a long time.

CHAPTER

8

BLAINE, BRYAN AND
"DOLLAR MARK" HANNA

November 10, 1880: Well, politics is full of surprises. Most folks believed the Republican nomination would be a toss-up between Grant and Blaine. It went to a dark horse, James A. Garfield, and now he's been elected.

May 1, 1894: Jacob Coxey and his ragged "army" marched into Washington to ask the government to begin a public works program to give relief to the thousands of men who have been jobless for the past several months. Coxey was arrested and the army disbanded, but at least he made some of those Washington politicians sit up and take notice of the plight we're in.

November 10, 1896: We've had one of the most interesting elections of our time. Thanks to the skillful maneuvering of "Dollar Mark" Hanna, it was won by Republican William McKinley, but it earned the respect of a lot of people for his opponent, William Jennings Bryan. Also, it marked the beginning of a new "Social Democratic" party, led by one Eugene V. Debs of Indiana, who, it is said, developed some interesting socialistic ideas while he was in prison.

THE "Greenback Labor" party held its first convention in June, 1880, in Chicago, where James B. Weaver of Iowa was nominated for the Presidency. Among its platform planks was one calling for a graduated income tax.

The old Greenback party might have died a natural death if it had not been for a series of railway strikes back in 1877, marked by battles between the strikers and armed troops. The labor unions, which were sympathetic with the aims of the Greenbackers, merged with them in 1878 to form the Greenback Labor party.

In the 1880 campaigns a clash of personalities split the Republican party into two camps and produced a Republican Presidential candidate who had not even tried to capture the nomination. During the Hayes administration the country was plagued by numerous strikes called by labor unions. Rich industrialists created huge trusts and monopolies, and in the booming West unscrupulous men were using crooked schemes to grab millions of acres of government homestead land. Although Hayes had done much to clean up corruption in government, he seemed unable to cope with these other problems, and as a result the Republican party lost more and more support from the voters.

One arm of the Republican party called itself "conservative" and was led by Senator Roscoe Conkling of New York. The other, "liberal," arm was headed by James G. Blaine, who had lost the Presidential nomination in 1876. Basically the differences between the two factions were minor. The real cause of the division was the personal dislike of Blaine and Conkling for each other. Conkling's conservatives were known as the "Stalwarts," Blaine's liberals as the "Half-Breeds."

At the Republican convention the strongest contenders for the Presidential nomination proved to be Ulysses S. Grant, James G. Blaine and John Sherman, Secretary of the Treasury.

In the first canvass, Grant led with 304 votes, Blaine was second with 284, and John Sherman a bad third with only 93. James Garfield of Ohio, who spearheaded Sherman's drive, delivered a forceful speech in behalf of Sherman as the candidate who could reunite the Republican party and win the election. In ballot after ballot the top three stayed in the same positions. The convention was deadlocked, although it seemed probable that Grant would eventually emerge as the winner.

A few delegations switched their votes to Sherman, but it soon became obvious that he could not win, and Sherman himself then sent a telegram urging the delegates to nominate Garfield! Garfield, more surprised than anyone, promptly announced that no one had the right to propose him as a candidate without his consent and that he would not agree to entering the race for the nomination.

In Garfield, however, the delegates saw a chance to break the convention deadlock. Ignoring his protest, they began a Garfield push by shifting fifty Blaine votes to Garfield on the thirty-fifth ballot. When a few other delegations also switched votes the Garfield bandwagon was rolling and enough delegates climbed aboard to bring it to the head of the parade. Like it or not, James A. Garfield was the Republican candidate for the Presidency in 1880. For the Vice Presidency the convention chose Chester A. Arthur, a New York politician who was a friend and associate of Roscoe Conkling.

In this election the Greenback Labor party polled more than a million votes and sent fourteen candidates to the House of Representatives, one of whom was Adlai E. Stevenson. He was the grandfather of Adlai Stevenson, the defeated Democratic nominee for the Presidency both in 1952 and 1956.

Garfield won the election, but on July 2, 1881, only four months after his inauguration, this man who hadn't sought the job, was shot in the back by Charles J. Guiteau, a disgruntled office-seeker, in a Washington railroad station. Critically wounded, Garfield was unable to perform his duties as President. To escape the oppressive Washington heat he was taken to a cottage in Elberon, New Jersey, but in the weeks that followed he was still too weak to perform the functions of his office, and the members of his Cabinet agreed that the Presidential duties should be delegated to Vice President Arthur. When they suggested that the wounded President should be informed of this proposal, his doctors warned that the shock of such news might kill Garfield, and for this reason no further action was taken.

President Garfield died on September 19 and Chester A. Arthur succeeded to the office.

The principal achievements in President Arthur's administration were the establishment of a Civil Service Commission and rules for appointing government employees; and a downward revision of the high protective tariff. In both of these fields there were opposing factions in the Republican and Democratic parties, and when the 1884 election campaigns approached, the outlook for another term for President Arthur was gloomy indeed. The Republicans turned for a third time to James G. Blaine.

The Greenback Labor party began to slump in the 1884 election campaigns. In that year the Anti-Monopoly party nominated General Benjamin F. Butler as its candidate for President, and the Greenback Labor party supported this nomination but had ceased to be a political power as a unit.

A new political nickname appeared in 1884—the "Mugwumps." The popular definition of "Mugwump" is "a bird who sits on a fence with his mug on one side and his wump on the other." Actually the word is believed to be a simplified version of *mugquomp*, used by the Algonquin Indians to denote a chief. It was used in 1884 as a term to describe disgruntled Republicans who tried to stop the nomination of James G. Blaine for the Presidency.

Blaine's campaign proved that sometimes a politician can be hurt by what he *doesn't* say. Blaine met with a group of Protestant ministers in New York who told him that they were not Mugwumps. "We are Republicans," one said, "and Republicans we will remain. We are loyal to you. We certainly will not support the party whose antecedents have been rum, Romanism and rebellion."

Blaine let this slap at the Democrats stand without protest, and when it was publicized in the press a great many Roman Catholics who had favored Blaine's election now saw him as anti-Catholic and switched to his opponent, Grover Cleveland, who became the first Democratic President to be elected after a twenty-four-year Republican reign.

When the Greenback Labor party lost its power and identity after the 1884 campaigns, disgruntled and restless farmers and laborers sought a new organization that could champion their causes. The farmers founded an association which they called the "Farmers' Alliance," and prepared a plan of attack that they hoped would get them some of the changes in laws and some of the improvements they wanted.

The next year, 1885, marked the birth of a new nickname for the Republican party—the "Grand Old Party," or G.O.P. for short. According to the Republican National Committee this term "came into general use in the United States about two decades after the Civil War, when the 'Grand Old Man' of England, William E. Gladstone, was at the acme of his fame. It is believed that Republican reference to their party by the affectionate term 'G.O.P.' was a somewhat spontaneous development from that nickname. Although the Democrats first took up the phrase 'G.O.P.' in derision, today the term is used by all persons of whatever party, without regard to the literal significance of the letters." Gladstone was twice Prime

Minister of Great Britain and was England's most outstanding statesman in the later half of the nineteenth century.

In 1890 the woman suffrage battlers, seeing strength in unity, combined the American with the National Woman Suffrage Association to form the "National American Woman Suffrage Association," with Elizabeth Stanton as president and Susan Anthony as vice president.

The women were often ridiculed by politicians who still insisted that woman's place was in the home. Among the jokes aimed at the ladies was one about two suffragettes who were jailed for disturbing the peace. In their cell one began to weep. "There, there, dear, you mustn't cry," the other said. "Just trust in God—She will protect us!"

On other political fronts the farmers continued to seek solutions to their own problems. Leaders of the Farmers' Alliance knew that to be effective they would have to wield strong political influence, so in 1891 the Alliance conceived and created a new "Populist" or "People's" party, aimed at serving the interests of both farm and labor.

Meeting in convention at Omaha, Nebraska, in 1892, the Populist party nominated General James B. Weaver of Iowa, a former Greenbacker, to be its Presidential candidate, and adopted a platform which blamed both Republicans and Democrats for all the injustices, corruption and ills of government. This excerpt from the party's platform shows the tone of the Populist charges:

> ... The newspapers are largely subsidized or muzzled; public opinion silenced; business prostrated; our homes covered with mortgages; labor impoverished; and the land concentrating in the hands of the capitalists. The urban workmen are denied the right of organization for self-protection; imported pauperized labor beats down their wages; a hireling standing army, unrecognized by our laws, is established to shoot them down ....

To correct these defects the Populists demanded a sound national currency, government ownership of railroads, telegraph and telephone lines, a graduated income tax, postal savings banks, an eight-hour workday and the unlimited free coinage of silver at a ratio of sixteen to one.

Free unlimited coinage of silver would mean that any person could take any quantity of silver to the United States Mint and have it made into coins without charge. The sixteen-to-one ratio would mean that sixteen parts (ounces, pounds, etc.) of silver would equal the value of one of the same parts of gold. Under such a system, holders of gold would undoubtedly hoard it, and silver would become the national currency.

Grover Cleveland opposed the "free-silverites" and stood for the single gold standard, under which all paper money or other legal tender was redeemable in specified quantities of gold as defined by law.

Attracting both farmers and factory workers, the Populist party soon mustered considerable voting strength. In some areas it was joined by Republicans, in others by Democrats. Although Democrat Grover Cleveland won the election in 1892, the Populists polled more than one million votes—sufficient evidence that this new party was not likely to fade away quickly.

Some goals of the Populist party—the graduated income tax, postal savings banks, the eight-hour workday—were to be reached by other political groups many years after Populism itself expired. Here again is evidence that minor political parties can and do strengthen our democratic system of government.

By 1894 the country was again in a serious economic depression. Business took a big slump and both wages and prices shot down. Thousands of workmen went on strike for higher pay and better working conditions, but manufacturers had few markets for goods and their plants closed up. Bands of hungry and desperate men who had lost homes and jobs roamed the towns and cities, living in leaky ramshackle huts without sanitary facilities, scavenging the countryside for food.

Jacob S. Coxey of Massillon, Ohio, organized and led to Washington the "Army of the Commonweal of Christ," comprising a thousand or more ragged and jobless men. Most were on foot, though some rode horseback or drove wagons. "General" Coxey proposed to have the government finance a nationwide roadbuilding program in which thousands of men could earn living wages. Coxey was labeled a "crackpot" by many, was arrested on May 1 for walking on the grass in the Capitol grounds, and was sentenced to serve twenty days in jail and to pay a five-dollar fine. "Coxey's Army" did not immediately attain its objective, but it did succeed in convincing many politicians and others that a public works program to relieve widespread unemployment should be a government responsibility.

A leader in a different cause stepped into the national political scene in 1895. In choosing satisfactory candidates for the Presidency, political parties as organized units have sometimes made their choices because of the influence of one man or perhaps a few men who push the buttons to make the party machinery click. Such a man was Marcus Alonzo ("Mark") Hanna of Ohio.

Mark Hanna was born in 1837 in New Lisbon, Ohio, the son of a wholesale grocer. As a child he moved to Cleveland and was educated in the Cleveland public schools and at Western Reserve University. He helped his father in the grocery business and eventually became a member of the firm, but after he married the daughter of Daniel P. Rhodes, a coal and iron merchant, young Hanna became Rhodes' partner, and by the time Mark was forty the business name was changed to M. A. Hanna & Company. Under Hanna's direction the firm bought and operated several coal and iron mines and built lake steamships in its own shipyards.

Adventurous, energetic and ambitious, Mark Hanna branched out in other directions. He went into banking, bought a newspaper, operated theaters and built up several street railway systems. To run his trolley cars he needed city franchises, and he proceeded to get them by paying substantial sums of money to city officials, an act which brought him into political circles. His payments were made openly, with no secrecy, and in time Hanna was in a position to give orders to the mayor and heads of city government bureaus in Cleveland, yet he used his power primarily to benefit the businessmen of the community.

In 1895, when Hanna was fifty-eight years old, his interest in national politics was greater than his interest in his business projects, most of which he left to the supervision of others while he waded into a campaign to make William McKinley, governor of Ohio, the next President of the United States.

The game of politics was not new to Hanna. A stanch Republican, he was convinced that only the Republican party had the know-how to run the country properly. He had been a delegate to two Republican conventions, had worked with McKinley, once saved McKinley from going bankrupt, and had such admiration for the governor that he devoted all of his remarkable talents to sending McKinley to the White House.

Hanna, who was made chairman of the Republican National Committee, rented a private railroad car to take McKinley to various cities where people could see and hear him.

He plastered billboards with posters proclaiming McKinley as the "advance agent of prosperity." He set out to convince prominent local Republicans in key cities that McKinley should be their candidate, but here he ran into obstacles. New England had a candidate of its own, and the two most powerful states, New York and Pennsylvania, were controlled by political "bosses," whom he wisely decided not to approach until he had built up stronger support for his friend.

Hanna's best bet appeared to be the South. Although it was a Democratic stronghold, the South would have more than two hundred delegates at the Republican national convention and they could wield considerable influence. Using the sugar-coated approach, Hanna brought McKinley to Georgia and staged a number of house parties to which he invited those southern Republicans who could do McKinley the most good. McKinley had a pleasing personality and an acceptable Republican attitude toward the issues of the day, and within a few weeks Hanna won the promise of support from the southerners he had entertained so lavishly.

Since the party-and-entertainment technique succeeded so well in the South, Hanna decided to repeat it in Cleveland, except that the guests were Republicans who had power in the West; and when they went home they were ready to use it in McKinley's behalf.

Just as Hanna had hoped and expected, the New York and Pennsylvania political bosses came to him to make a deal. If McKinley, as President, would make certain appointments, they would line up their delegates on his side. McKinley, however, refused to consider any such agreement.

To oppose McKinley for the Presidency the Democrats, with Populist support, favored William Jennings Bryan of Illinois, an attorney and former member of Congress. As in

1892, a major issue in the contest was gold versus silver. The Republicans favored the gold standard and the Democrats and Populists wanted the unlimited coinage of silver.

Even as a youth, Bryan had made such eloquent speeches that he was known as "The Boy Orator of the River Platte." One of his Republican opponents now recalled that nickname and commented, "Don't forget that the River Platte is only four feet deep and five miles wide at the mouth!"

At the Democratic national convention in Chicago, Bryan, a spellbinding orator and champion of free coinage of silver, made what was probably the most famous speech in his career. Climaxed by the ringing cry, "You shall not press down upon the brow of labor this crown of thorns, you shall not crucify mankind upon a cross of gold!" the address became known as Bryan's "Cross of Gold" speech, and it went far towards winning him the Democratic nomination.

Bryan could give as well as take. Speaking to an informal gathering of farmers in Omaha, Nebraska, he stood on a manure-spreader so the crowd could see him. He laughed and said, "This is the first time I have ever spoken from a Republican platform!"

Many Democrats who opposed the free coinage of silver bolted the party and formed the "National Democratic" party, held their own convention in Indianapolis, Indiana, and wrote a platform favoring the gold standard. This split in the Democratic ranks merely served to strengthen the Republicans.

Mark Hanna was out to win. Called "Dollar Mark" by some, not only did he contribute about $100,000 of his own to his campaign for McKinley, but he also persuaded numerous businessmen and big corporations to donate hundreds of thousands more. He printed and distributed millions of copies of vote-for-McKinley pamphlets, thousands of posters, produced campaign buttons and other souvenirs, and staged all sorts of rallies and parades for his candidate.

The Republican slogan was "A full dinner pail," a cry that had a strong appeal for hungry people. It was also an echo of one used effectively in the Harrison–Van Buren campaign of 1840: "Van's policy—fifty cents a day and French soup; our policy, two dollars a day and roast beef!"

As for McKinley's own role, Hanna conceived a new idea for campaigning. Instead of having the candidate rush around the country making speeches, he had McKinley remain at home in Canton, Ohio, where groups of delegates and voters met and talked with him in what was called "the front porch campaign."

In the midst of this activity a new group, the "Social Democratic" party, held a national convention for the first time and nominated Eugene V. Debs of Terre Haute, Indiana, as its Presidential choice.

Debs had left school when he was fifteen to work as a locomotive fireman and later as a grocery clerk. When he was only twenty, he helped to organize a labor union, the Brotherhood of Locomotive Firemen, and became its secretary. At twenty-four he was elected City Clerk of Terre Haute, and in 1885 became a member of the Indiana legislature.

A few years later Debs helped to establish the American Railway Union, of which he became president. His policies won him considerable recognition in 1894 after the union won a battle with the Great Northern Railroad for higher wages, and shortly afterwards Debs' union helped striking employees of the Pullman Company in Chicago by halting the movements of Pullman cars.

This action landed Debs in hot water. President Cleveland

sent federal troops into Chicago to get trains rolling, and a federal grand jury indicted Debs and others for interfering with the United States mails. They were also charged with contempt of court in violating an injunction against the strikers, and on the contempt charge Debs and six associates were sentenced to serve six months in prison.

For lack of other activity, Debs devoted most of the six months in his prison cell to reading about politics and government. He was deeply impressed by what he read about socialism, and when the prison doors opened and he was set free, Debs had become a confirmed Socialist.

Basically the Socialist cause advocated the public ownership of industries producing goods needed by all the people, such industries not to be operated for profit. In addition Debs and his party urged adoption of a form of social security, payment of an income tax, voting rights for women, unemployment relief and a law to forbid child labor. A major point was that all of the social reforms proposed by the Socialists must be achieved by peaceful means, not by violence.

After his release Debs founded the "Social Democratic Party of America" and entered the Presidential race against McKinley and Bryan.

The Populist party, unable to settle upon a candidate of its own, chose to support Bryan along with the Democrats.

The Prohibition party stepped into the fray with its forces divided. One faction, the "Narrow Gaugers," demanded a platform with only one familiar plank: Down with the making and selling of intoxicating liquors. The other faction, the "Broad Gaugers," wanted several planks in the platform, and since the two groups could not agree they went their separate ways, each nominating a candidate of its own.

When the 1896 campaigns ended and the votes were in,

Bryan was defeated, the Socialists polled only a handful of votes, the Populist party was on the way to extinction and the Prohibitionists had to regroup their forces for the next race. McKinley was the victor by a margin of more than half a million popular votes and ninety-five electoral votes.

With the wealthy industrialists supporting McKinley, factory fires were already burning again, wages and prices were rising and the promise of "a full dinner pail" seemed about to materialize. The outlook for the country and the new administration was bright and cheerful.

Happiest of all was Mark Hanna, for he had successfully manufactured a President.

CHAPTER

9

FROM TEDDY ROOSEVELT TO TEAPOT DOME

September 14, 1901: President McKinley died today as the result of the shooting at Buffalo, and Vice President Theodore Roosevelt has assumed the Presidency. "Boss" Platt must be pretty upset, but most folks are happy to have Teddy in The White House. The old "Rough Rider" is a go-getter, and we're likely to see sparks fly during his administration.

November 19, 1912: Nearly four years ago Teddy Roosevelt picked William Howard Taft as his own Republican successor. Later, Teddy didn't agree with Taft's policies, so he headed a new "Bull Moose" party to compete with both Democrats and Republicans. He pulled a lot of votes, but not enough, for this election went to Democrat Woodrow Wilson, a college professor who has promised to make a host of progressive reforms in government.

December 31, 1919: This year has seen important history in the making. After the Allies won the World War, President Wilson worked himself into a paralytic stroke trying to win support for U. S. membership in the League of Nations, but the opposition led by Republican Senator Henry Cabot Lodge was much too great. Also, we now have a federal law against the sale and use of intoxicating liquors. This makes the Prohibition party happy, but we may find that we can't legislate against a lot of people who like a nip now and then. For one more historic milestone, Congress has submitted a new Constitutional amendment (the 19th) to the states for ratification. This would give women the right to vote, and it looks as if they'll get it.

The American battleship *Maine* rode at anchor in Havana Harbor on February 15, 1898, stationed there to observe and report developments in a violent Cuban revolution. At 9:40 that night a terrific explosion rocked the city—the *Maine* was blown to pieces and went down with 252 men. Eight others later died of wounds.

No one knows exactly what caused the explosion. A Naval Board of Inquiry declared that a submerged mine had blown up. The Spaniards claimed the blast originated inside the ship and was accidental. Whatever its cause, the tragedy was the climax to a series of differences between Cuba and the United States that resulted in the Spanish-American War.

Fighting in that war was young Theodore Roosevelt, who had been Assistant Secretary of the Navy in President McKinley's Cabinet.

As a boy, Teddy Roosevelt was so frail and sickly that he was unable to play ordinary games with other children or to attend the public schools. He read a great deal and liked to collect specimens of butterflies and insects for study. His father and various instructors taught him to hunt, to box and to ride horseback, and gradually this kind of exercise built him into a strong and vigorous young man.

In the Spanish-American War, Roosevelt assembled and commanded the First U. S. Volunteer Cavalry, made up mostly of rugged cowboys from the West. In one of the most famous Cuban battles, the Battle of San Juan Hill, Roosevelt led his "Rough Riders" across a valley and up the slopes of Kettle Hill to capture an outpost on the main Spanish defense line.

After the war he was welcomed home as a swashbuckling hero and as a Republican was elected governor of the State of New York. He attacked what he called "big business," imposed taxes on large corporations, made promotions and appointments on the basis of merit instead of political connections, sponsored laws to help the working class and to preserve forests and wildlife.

Roosevelt's fight against powerful business interests and in behalf of the common people made him an enemy of Thomas C. Platt, who was the Republican political boss of New York State at that time. When Roosevelt decided to seek another term as governor, Platt schemed to have him nominated as the Republican party's candidate for Vice President, a running mate for William McKinley who was up for a second term as President. Roosevelt fought against the nomination, but when thousands of his western friends cheered and encouraged him, he decided to accept it.

Boss Tom Platt's maneuver had been designed to get rid of Roosevelt as governor and to push him into obscurity as Vice President.

It was during this Presidential battle that Eugene Debs' Social Democratic party merged with the Socialist Labor party and soon afterwards became the "Socialist Party of America."

Boss Platt's anti-Roosevelt plan misfired. McKinley was re-elected, but on September 6, 1901, he was shot by a madman at a reception in Buffalo, New York, died eight days later, and Theodore Roosevelt at forty-two became the youngest man yet to serve as President of the United States.

As President he launched an attack on the moneyed interests (he called them "Wall Street") and through the courts he broke up powerful corporations, not because they were too big but because their dealings were unscrupulous. He cracked down on firms that were making and selling foods and medicines that contained harmful ingredients, and he also struck at those labor unions which tried to solve their problems by violence. As a conservationist he increased forest preserves by millions of acres and assigned Secret Service agents to investigate and arrest western cattle barons who stole millions of acres of government lands that were intended to be the farms and ranches of homesteaders.

"The things that will destroy America," Roosevelt said, "are prosperity at any price, peace at any price, safety first instead of duty first, the love of soft living, and the get-rich-quick theory of life."

Roosevelt brought about so many reforms in government and business, all in behalf of the people, that the Populist party lost the reasons for its existence and faded into obscurity.

In his foreign policy Roosevelt followed his own advice: "Speak softly, but carry a big stick!" He sent the United States Navy on a world voyage to show other countries the might of America's sea power, and he led the actions that brought about the building of the Panama Canal.

Roosevelt won a second term as President with a huge margin of votes, but in 1909 he refused another nomination and was succeeded by his own Republican choice, William Howard Taft.

After he left the White House, Roosevelt and his son Kermit made a scientific expedition to Africa for The Smithsonian Institution, hunting big game and collecting specimens for the museum. When he came home in June, 1910, he found that there was a bitter struggle going on between factions of the Republican party, and his friends urged him to become a candidate for President again. Roosevelt disagreed with many of President Taft's policies, and after some deliberation he said, "All right—my hat is in the ring."

At the Republican convention in 1912 certain politicians

wanted to make "deals" to assure Roosevelt's nomination, but on terms he said he could not accept. He was opposed to Taft as a candidate, but was willing to compromise on some other Republican leader if the party would throw out certain delegates who, he claimed, had been appointed by fraud.

The leaders would not agree and Taft was nominated, so Teddy Roosevelt and his followers broke loose from the Republicans and formed the "Progressive" party, with Roosevelt as its Presidential candidate and Hiram W. Johnson, governor of California, for the Vice Presidency.

At the convention, in answer to reporters' questions about his health, Roosevelt said, "I'm as strong as a bull moose." The newspapers picked up the term, labeled the Progressives as the "Bull Moose" party, and a bull moose became the cartoonists' symbol for the Progressive party.

It was during this campaign that Theodore Roosevelt, on his way to address a crowd in Milwaukee, Wisconsin, was shot by John Schrank, a fanatic who wanted to prevent Roosevelt from serving a third term as President. With Schrank's bullet still in his right breast and bleeding profusely Roosevelt insisted upon delivering his speech, and almost two hours passed before he agreed to go to a hospital for treatment of his wound.

The Democratic party, convening in Baltimore, nominated Woodrow Wilson, governor of New Jersey, and the race was on. Wilson emerged the winner, with Roosevelt second and Taft third.

Woodrow Wilson, attorney at law, professor of history and political economy, and former president of Princeton University, was a quiet man who showed himself to be an able politician. His dignified professorial bearing hid a warm and human side that frequently showed itself to close friends, and to members of his Secret Service bodyguard. Once when the President and a lone Secret Service agent rode slowly through a Washington park, they passed a small boy sitting beside the road.

"Did you see what that boy did?" the President asked.

"No, sir, I didn't," the agent said.

"He made a face at me."

"Oh? Well, sir—"

"Know what I did?" the President interrupted. "I made a worse face right back at him!" Both men laughed.

The Wilson administration achieved many notable advances. The protective tariff was lowered, an income tax law was passed, the Federal Reserve System was established, and anti-trust and trade laws were enacted to fight monopolies and unfair trade methods of powerful corporations. The federal government contributed money equal to sums provided by the states for improvements in agriculture, education and roadbuilding. Virtually all of these were reforms that Wilson had promised to make.

In June, 1914, during Wilson's first term, the Archduke Francis Ferdinand of Austria was assassinated in Sarajevo, and within a few weeks World War I began in Europe. The United States took a neutral position, and when the 1916 elections approached, Wilson campaigned for a second term on the slogan, "He kept us out of war."

For the 1916 Presidential battle the Progressive (Bull Moose) party again nominated Theodore Roosevelt. Knowing that he would not have the support of the regular Republican party, Roosevelt later withdrew his name as a candidate and urged his followers to back the Republican nominee, Charles Evans Hughes, associate justice of the Supreme Court and former governor of New York. The Progressive party thus faded away.

Hughes traveled about the country attacking Wilson's domestic policies, while Wilson made only a few public appearances and let the Democrats hammer home the slogan, "He kept us out of war." In California, Mr. Justice Hughes' appearances and meetings with political leaders were set up by Republican Committeeman William H. Crocker. Relations between Crocker and California's Governor Hiram Johnson were so deplorable that Crocker deliberately prevented a meeting between Johnson and Hughes. Candidate Hughes' failure to pay even a courtesy call on the governor was virtually an open insult to Johnson.

On Election Night in 1916 a Republican victory seemed assured. Hughes needed 266 electoral votes to win, and he already had captured 254. With the 13 electoral votes of California, he would have a total of 267. New York newspapers rushed extras to the streets announcing that Hughes had been elected, and there was singing and dancing at Republican headquarters.

Sometime after midnight a newspaper reporter knocked on the door of Mr. Hughes' hotel suite. The door was opened by one of Hughes' associates.

"I'd like to see Mr. Justice Hughes," the reporter said. "I presume he'd like to make a statement about—"

"Not now, old man. You'll have to wait until morning. *The President* has gone to bed."

The reporter grinned. "Oh, I see. Well, you tell him when he wakes up that *President* Wilson has been re-elected, will you? Good night."

It was true. Thanks to the influence of Governor Hiram Johnson and Hughes' failure to meet with him during the campaign, the electoral vote of California went to Woodrow Wilson and took the Presidency away from the man who went to bed confident that he had won it.

America's neutrality did not last long. In March, 1917, German submarines sank three American ships. On April 2 President Wilson asked Congress to declare war on Germany and uttered the famous words, "The world must be made safe for democracy!"

The Socialist party not only took a firm stand against the fighting, but also attacked the United States government on the grounds that it was arresting and persecuting people wrongly charged with sedition. Socialist leader Eugene Debs was one of the nation's most bitter critics, and his outbursts were so strong that he was arrested, indicted and tried for violating the Espionage Act and was sentenced in September, 1918, to serve ten years in a federal prison.

During the Wilson administration the Eighteenth Amendment to the Constitution was ratified (January, 1919) by three-fourths of the states. This amendment prohibited the manufacture, sale, importation, exportation or transportation of intoxicating liquors, and although national prohibition became a reality under a Democratic regime it was clearly a victory for the Prohibition party.

Despite its poor showings in national elections, the Prohibition party had earlier helped to achieve prohibition in several "dry" states. Organizations such as the Women's Christian Temperance Union, the Anti-Saloon League, the National Temperance Society, and the Total Abstinence Brotherhood brought their influence to bear upon the state lawmakers to forbid the making and selling of wine, beer and liquor.

The Prohibition party also endorsed the woman suffrage

movement, which was gathering strength from many other sources. With the World War raging in Europe, American women had performed men's jobs while the men were at the front, and Congress developed a new appreciation of women. The House of Representatives took a vote on woman suffrage, but the voice of opposition was still loud and it was imperative that every possible favorable vote be counted. Three representatives who were in hospitals left their sickbeds to vote for the measure. Another had to be carried into the House on a stretcher. One rushed all the way from the Pacific Coast to vote in time, and still another came from the deathbed of his wife, who was an ardent suffragist. The vote was 274 to 136 in favor of the measure—a fraction of one vote over the required two-thirds!

Now the question went to the Senate, which put up a battle to keep the measure from coming to a vote at all, but the women and their suffrage allies, including several state legislatures, exerted so much pressure that the Senate was forced to consider the bill. The Senate voted 62 for, 34 against —two votes short of a Constitutional majority. In February, 1919, the Senate voted again, with 63 for and 33 against—just one vote short!

The Sixty-sixth Congress met in special session in May, 1919. The pressures increased. Parades, speeches, printed propaganda and other tactics paid off, for Congress, on June 4, 1919, agreed to submit to the states the Nineteenth (Equal Rights) Amendment to the Constitution. Its major provision was that no citizen should be deprived of the right to vote because of sex.

As the woman suffrage fight ended with victory in sight in 1919, a different kind of battle began—a campaign to organize a League of Nations designed to settle international differences by peaceful negotiation rather than the force of arms. Woodrow Wilson put up a hard and brave fight to have the United States join the League, but he was bitterly opposed by powerful political interests, including a group of senators led by Republican Henry Cabot Lodge.

Senator Lodge, a powerful foe of President Wilson and his policies, spearheaded the attack against American membership in the League and was supported by Republican Senators Hiram Johnson, William Borah and other "isolationists." The League of Nations, established by the Treaty of Versailles, proposed to insure peace by requiring member nations to reduce armament, to mediate disputes, to make social and economic improvements where needed, to respect each other's domain and, if necessary, to pool resources to punish any member country that sought to disturb world peace.

Some of the reasons Senator Lodge and his followers opposed membership in the League were that it might interfere with the right of Congress to declare war; that it could involve the United States in European wars; that the League probably would be dominated by the British. Also, the Republicans were antagonized by the fact that Wilson and his Democratic advisers had failed to include any Republican senators or representatives in the President's official participation in the peace conference, and that Wilson had failed to make open protests at the conference about many aspects of the peace treaty that were considered unjust and unnecessary. In other words, political party opposition was an important factor in the anti-League fight.

Although he was weak and exhausted, Wilson disregarded doctors' warnings and set out on a speaking tour to plead for the direct support of the people of the United States for his peace program. His plea was that without full support of the

League, another world war was inevitable. In September, 1919, he collapsed in Colorado and was brought back to Washington partially paralyzed. He received no visitors and it was commonly reported that a small group of his close associates was led by Mrs. Wilson in carrying on her disabled husband's Presidential duties. No move was made to designate Vice President Thomas Marshall as "Acting President."

Marshall himself had little respect for the Vice Presidency and enjoyed telling a joke about a family with two sons. "One boy went to sea," he would say, "and the other became Vice President of the United States. Neither was ever heard from again!"

Woodrow Wilson had sacrificed himself in vain, for America refused to become a member of the League of Nations.

In October, 1919, Congress passed the National Prohibition Act, known as the Volstead Act, providing for the enforcement of the Eighteenth Amendment. President Wilson vetoed the measure, but Congress overrode the veto.

The Prohibitionists considered the new law a great boon to society. Workmen could no longer squander their hard-earned wages in saloons or in buying liquor instead of food and other family necessities. Mental and physical health would be improved. Children and parents would gain greater respect for each other, and families would enjoy higher living standards in more comfortable homes.

Although these goals were reached in some quarters, Prohibition plunged the nation into a new and violent era. New words appeared in American vocabularies—*bootlegger, gangster, racketeer, speakeasy, gun-moll, hijack.* Juniper juice was mixed with illicit alcohol in bathtubs and called "bathtub gin." Home-made beer was "spiked" with ether. Unscrupulous bootleggers sold drinks made from wood alcohol or other poisons, often blinding or killing the buyers who drank the stuff. Smugglers grew prosperous and many law-enforcement officers turned crooked, accepting liberal "payoffs" in return for neglecting their duty.

During this period the Socialist party organized small Socialist clubs whose members were mostly Europeans speaking a common language. Several of these groups, favoring the Russian brand of Communism, moved to have the party tie in immediately to the Communist Third International (the Comintern) and become an out-and-out Communist party. Other radicals wanted to wait until the Socialist party's convention in August, 1919, to try to swing its members to the Communist line. The result was that these two radical groups separated from the Socialists. The first group established the Communist party, the second organized the Communist Labor party.

Almost immediately the Attorney General of the United States cracked down on the "Reds," raided their offices, placed many under arrest and ordered scores deported from the United States. Under this withering attack, the remaining members went "underground" to continue their activities in secrecy.

While the major political parties were on the firing line for the 1920 Presidential election battle, the women of America finally emerged as victors in the fight for suffrage that had begun some seventy years earlier. On August 26, 1920, the states ratified the Nineteenth Amendment, giving the women the right to vote. For the first time, thousands of women would lawfully cast ballots for Presidential candidates.

To help them make wise use of their voting power, Carrie Chapman Catt and the National American Woman Suffrage Association formed a "League of Women Voters" as a volunteer non-partisan, non-profit organization whose goal was "to promote political responsibility through informed and active participation of citizens in government." It is still an active organization to this day.

By encouraging its members to work as individuals in the political parties of their choice and to keep informed about candidates and important issues, the League expects members to avoid any similarity to the woman who told a friend, "I voted this morning. The only trouble was that I didn't know anything about anybody on the ballot, so I just voted for all the Irish names!"

At the 1920 conventions the Democrats nominated Governor James M. Cox of Ohio for the Presidency, and a young New Yorker named Franklin Delano Roosevelt as his running mate.

Although Eugene Debs was serving a federal prison sentence, he was again nominated for the Presidency by the Socialist party.

When the Republican convention opened, the principal contenders for the Presidential nomination were Senator Hiram Johnson of California, Governor Frank O. Lowden of Illinois, and General Leonard Wood. There were some hopes that Herbert Hoover, who had served as Food Administrator during the war, might be the choice of the delegates, but there was no such general feeling about Warren G. Harding, an Ohio newspaper publisher.

Harding's nomination was masterminded by Harry M. Daugherty of Ohio, a shrewd politician, who, like "Dollar Mark" Hanna, was skilled in the kind of maneuvering needed to put his choice in the top spot. When a newspaper reporter questioned Daugherty about the outcome of the Republican convention, he showed all the attributes of a successful fortune-teller and proved that Harding's nomination was a foregone conclusion.

Prophesied Daugherty, "The convention will be deadlocked and after the other candidates have gone their limit, some twelve or fifteen men, worn out and bleary-eyed for lack of sleep, will sit down about two o'clock in the morning in a smoke-filled room in some hotel and decide the nomination. When that time comes, Harding will be selected."

The prediction was correct. The convention was deadlocked, a group of bleary-eyed politicians led by Senator Henry Cabot Lodge met in a room in the Blackstone Hotel in Chicago, and in a cloud of cigar and cigarette smoke decided that Harding would be the Republican dark-horse candidate. Calvin Coolidge of Vermont was nominated for the Vice Presidency. Daugherty's phrase, "a smoke-filled room," became famous in the language of politics.

Harding won the 1920 election, but many politicians were surprised to discover that Socialist Eugene Debs, locked in a jail cell, polled more than one million votes.

In 1921 the "underground" Communists blossomed out under a new name—the "Workers'" party—led by William Z. Foster, later known as "the American Lenin."

When Harding stepped into the White House, the growing crime wave born of prohibition was soon rivaled by one born of crooked politics, and the Harding administration was marred by extensive frauds and scandals.

Harry Daugherty, who had managed Harding's campaign, was appointed Attorney General, and it was not long before he and other close and trusted friends of the President were accused of selling their influence. The Secretary of the Interior accepted a huge bribe to lease government-owned oil lands to private oil companies, a scheme that became known as the Teapot Dome oil scandal.

Investigations indicated that although President Harding must have had some inkling of the wrongdoing of his associates, he did not realize until too late that they were betraying him on a grand scale.

In 1923 the President made a trip to Alaska. In San Francisco, on the way back to Washington, he became seriously ill. On August 2, after five days under the care of doctors in the Palace Hotel in San Francisco, Mr. Harding died.

At two o'clock on the morning of August 3 Vice President Calvin Coolidge was awakened at the Vermont farmhouse of his father, where he had been spending a vacation. In the little parlor of the house, in the dim light of a kerosene lamp, the Presidential oath of office was administered to Mr. Coolidge by his father, a justice of the peace. Calvin Coolidge had inherited the Presidency, and with it the festering sores of corruption and knavery that may have helped to drive Harding to his death.

CHAPTER

10

THE BIG SLUMP, THE NEW DEAL AND "IKE"

March 6, 1927: The country was never more prosperous. President Coolidge, who took over when Warren Harding died in 1923, has acted with good old Yankee shrewdness, but now he insists he "does not choose to run" as the Republican candidate in 1928. We will need someone who can keep the prosperity pot boiling.

November 10, 1929: The prosperity pot has boiled over and put out the fire. The bottom has dropped out of our whole economic system, and President Hoover's campaign promise to banish poverty is as empty as most pocketbooks. Jobless and hungry people are desperate and a lot of them are turning to the Communist party, which seeks to take over all private property, through violence if necessary. What's to be done? What? What?

March 6, 1933: Our new Democratic President, Franklin D. Roosevelt, is a man of action. Only hours after taking office he has declared a bank holiday and is planning a tremendous public works program to put people back to work. We're to have a "new deal," he says.

January 20, 1953: A military hero who once said he was not equipped to become President was inaugurated today. General Dwight D. (Ike) Eisenhower will have his hands full and may wish he was back in the army! He's our first Republican President since FDR was elected in 1932. We saw FDR break all records by being elected four times, we've had a "Fair Deal" under Harry Truman, and a war in Korea that's still going on. Everybody hopes that Ike can end the fighting.

When Calvin Coolidge moved into the White House his first task was to battle the influence peddlers, the cheats and the schemers he inherited from the Harding administration. As he "cleaned house" he gradually succeeded in regaining public respect for his Republican party.

Economically the country was booming. Thousands of new automobiles were rolling off the assembly lines, new roads were being built across the country, and the average worker was buying furniture, appliances, cars and other luxuries (or necessities) on the installment plan. As one mechanic said, "I'm living better than I ever did before—and all for a dollar down and a sheriff a month!"

Surrounded by such prosperity, President Coolidge found it prudent to sit quietly and let things hum. He had so little to say that newspapers called him "Silent Cal." Indeed he was noted for his economy of words, and there are many stories on that subject.

One is that when he first became President a messenger from the Treasury Department was sent to the White House to hand Mr. Coolidge his first Presidential pay check. The messenger's supervisor said, "When you give this to the President, I want you to remember everything he says and come back and tell me about it."

The messenger was ushered into the President's office, where he handed the pay check to Mr. Coolidge. "Silent Cal" merely nodded, put the check on his desk and began to read some correspondence, but the Treasury messenger didn't move. The President looked up at him as though to say, "Well? What do you want?" but Cal said not a word.

"Mr. President," the messenger said, "begging your pardon, sir, but my boss told me I should tell him whatever you said when I gave you your check—and you ain't said nothin' yet."

The President smiled faintly, glanced at the check and replied, "Come again!"

The 1924 campaigns offered little excitement. Coolidge was nominated by the Republicans, with Charles G. Dawes, a Chicago banker, as their Vice Presidential candidate.

The Democrats nominated John W. Davis of West Virginia, a lawyer, and Governor Charles Bryan of Nebraska, a brother of William Jennings Bryan. They attacked the Republicans for the corruption in the Harding administration and advocated repeal of the Eighteenth Amendment and membership in the League of Nations.

The Republicans pointed to the nation's prosperity and adopted the slogan, "Keep Cool With Coolidge." They were confident of victory, but they met some determined opposition from an unexpected quarter.

A new "Progressive" party, sponsored by the "Conference for Progressive Political Action," nominated Senator Robert ("Battling Bob") LaFollette of Wisconsin as the Progressive candidate for the Presidency. The strength of this party came primarily from discontented farmers and from labor organizations who believed the government was favoring big business and industry to the detriment of farm and labor.

Bushy-haired, dynamic Robert LaFollette, a former governor of Wisconsin, was an isolationist who had voted against American participation in World War I and in the League of Nations. He was, however, a champion of the rights of the farmer and the small businessman, and a foe of the monopolists, big business interests, the political bosses, and those who sought to strip the country of its forests and plunder its other natural resources. In many respects his ideals were similar to those of Thomas Jefferson, and he had been just as ardent a patriot.

For the first time in history, the powerful American Federation of Labor endorsed a Presidential candidate—LaFollette—and he also won the support of the Socialist party. In the election LaFollette received almost five million popular votes, but he lost to Coolidge, and soon after the Republican victory the Conference for Progressive Political Action went out of business.

The prosperity boom rolled forward under Coolidge. The installment fever had its counterpart in the stock market, where investors gambled heavily and bought stocks "on margin," paying a percentage of the real cost and selling (or hoping to sell) at a handsome profit.

In 1927 when people began to talk about candidates for the Presidential election of 1928, Mr. Coolidge wrote a one-sentence memorandum which he gave to newspaper reporters: "I do not choose to run for President in nineteen twenty-eight."

The Republican leaders failed to change his mind and scurried around to find another candidate. Among three or four possibilities the strongest contender seemed to be Herbert Hoover, Secretary of Commerce, and when the Republican convention was held in Kansas City in June, 1928, Hoover was nominated on the first ballot.

At Houston, Texas, Franklin D. Roosevelt made a stirring speech nominating Alfred E. Smith, Governor of New York, as the Democratic candidate for the Presidency, and called Smith "The Happy Warrior."

A vital issue in the 1928 campaigns was Prohibition, and although both parties agreed that the liquor laws should be enforced, Al Smith favored modification of the laws.

THE BIG SLUMP, THE NEW DEAL AND "IKE" 149

An even greater issue, however, was the fact that Smith was a Roman Catholic—and the seeds of "nativism" that sprouted and grew in the anti-Catholic riots of the 1840s were once again pushing into view. Smith's opponents began a whispering campaign warning the voters that if he were elected the United States would be controlled by the Pope in Rome. Candidate Hoover vigorously denounced this kind of political warfare, but just as in the earlier anti-Catholic movements the rumor-makers had done their work well and when the votes were counted Hoover was elected by a landslide. Of course bigotry alone did not defeat Smith, who received more than 40 per cent of the popular vote. The promise of continued prosperity held a tremendous appeal, but the religious propaganda against Smith was considered to have turned a great many people away from him.

In politics, as in other fields, history often repeats itself. William McKinley's promise of "A full dinner pail" cropped up again in Hoover's campaign speeches: "The slogan of progress is changing from the full dinner pail to the full garage." Also, when Martin Van Buren succeeded Andrew Jackson in 1837 there was a prosperity boom which turned to a bust soon after Van Buren took office, but the economic depression of Van Buren's time was like a penny in the Mint compared to the disaster that was to overtake the nation under Hoover.

At his inauguration in 1929 Mr. Hoover did not take the oath of office as President, because the taking of oaths was contrary to his religious precepts as a Quaker. Instead, he made an "affirmation"—a solemn declaration equivalent to an oath.

In 1929 it appeared that President Hoover's campaign prediction that "poverty will be banished from the nation" would come true. Big business was still thriving and people were making fortunes overnight in the stock market. However, wages for the average worker rose very little, and farm prices were so low that farmers suffered. Factories were glutting the market with all kinds of consumer goods, but buying slowed down and the goods piled up. In October, 1929, the whole bottom dropped out of the prosperity basket.

Stock prices took a dive, speculators could not meet their payments, thousands of firms went bankrupt, factories closed their gates and shut down their machinery, millions of Americans lost jobs and had no money to buy goods, and those who were lucky enough to work were paid wages that were barely enough to buy food and pay the rent. Jobless men, many of whom had once been prosperous, sold apples on the streets for five cents each, with few customers. Thousands stood in lines to get soup or bread. Banks went out of business and there were frequent instances of desperate men jumping to their deaths from the roofs or upper floors of tall buildings.

Like "Coxey's Army" on a bigger scale, and reminiscent of Shays' Rebellion in 1787, thousands of unemployed war veterans descended on Washington in a "bonus march" to persuade Congress to pay military bonuses before they were due. Most of these jobless men lived in squalor in improvised shacks and tents in a Washington area that became known as "Hooverville."

Congress provided money to send the men back to their homes, and many accepted the offer. Others who refused to go were driven out of Washington by American troops, led by General Douglas MacArthur and a young major named Dwight D. Eisenhower.

Such conditions were ideal for recruiting new members of the "Workers'" party, the enemy of capitalism. This organization changed its name in 1929 to "The Communist Party of the United States of America," and in 1930 elected as its general secretary Kansas-born Earl R. Browder, who had helped to organize the Communist party in this country.

President Hoover pleaded in vain with manufacturers to stop discharging their employees. At the same time he told the country that prosperity was "just around the corner"; that bad times would soon end and that business and industry would return to normal. But the bad times grew worse, and Mr. Hoover and his party seemed at a loss to cope with the situation. Not until he approached the end of his term did he move toward aggressive action. Congress passed a law establishing the Reconstruction Finance Corporation, through which the government would lend substantial sums of money to states, cities, banks, farm groups and railroads, to get the national economy rolling once more.

With another election soon due, the Republicans nominated Mr. Hoover for a second term. Their platform skipped lightly over the depression, skirted the issue of Prohibition, and offered no down-to-earth recommendations for getting the nation back on its economic feet.

The leading Democratic contenders were Al Smith and New York's Governor Franklin D. Roosevelt. Smith had lost the last election and the party leaders felt that his religious affiliation would again hurt his chances, so the nomination went to Roosevelt.

In his acceptance speech at Chicago, Mr. Roosevelt championed the cause of "the forgotten man" and pledged himself and his party to "a new deal for the American people." The party presented a bold program for national recovery and endorsed the repeal of the Prohibition laws.

Minor political parties also campaigned in 1932. The Socialist candidate was Norman Thomas; the Socialist Labor party's hope was Verne L. Reynolds of Maryland; the Communist party runner was William Z. Foster, and William D. Upshaw of Georgia carried the banner for the Prohibition party.

Six states voted for Hoover. The other forty-two chose Roosevelt, with the usual smattering for the minor candidates.

After Hoover's defeat he invited Roosevelt to the White House to discuss the economic, social and international problems of the day. Mr. Roosevelt went and listened politely, but said in effect that President Hoover's troubles were (as yet) none of Roosevelt's business, and he offered no constructive advice.

Mr. Roosevelt's inauguration in 1933 was the last to be held on March 4. The Twentieth Amendment to the Constitution, ratified in 1933, set January 20 as Inauguration Day, thus eliminating the "lame ducks"—the representatives and senators who had failed to be re-elected, but who had remained in office from election day in November to the following March 4.

President Roosevelt's troubleshooting began within hours after his inauguration. He ordered all banks closed, and those that were unsound remained closed. Many of the others later reopened with deposits insured by the government up to $5000 (subsequently raised to $10,000). With the cooperation of Congress he set up new government agencies designed to put people back to work in droves—agencies such as the Civil Works Administration (CWA), the Works Progress Administration (WPA), the Public Works Administration (PWA), and the Federal Emergency Relief Administration (FERA). Some of these gave federal money to states, cities and towns (called "pump priming" in political parlance) to help the unemployed. Some mapped out projects for building roads, power plants, dams and other construction that would create jobs at living wages and also bring improvements to the land.

Like some of his predecessors, including Jackson and Hoover, Roosevelt assembled a group of advisers who were popularly known as "Brain Trusters," and who helped him prepare and execute many bold plans to aid national recovery.

In 1933 the Twenty-first Amendment to the Constitution repealed the Eighteenth Amendment, and Prohibition ended. New laws were passed to relieve distressed farmers and to make it possible for home-owners to get loans at low interest. Congress imposed strict legal regulations upon stock exchanges and dealers in securities to forestall another stock market crash like that of 1929. A Civilian Conservation Corps (CCC) employed thousands of young men from city slums to plant forests, build dams, and otherwise help to conserve natural resources. Despite powerful opposition, the Social Security Administration was established to provide retirement income and survivors' insurance for the elderly. Roosevelt's "New Deal" for social progress was in full swing, and the national economy was definitely on the rise.

The nation's recovery under Roosevelt's forceful leadership made him an easy winner in the 1936 elections. In his inaugural address on January 20, 1937, he promised to continue his fight, saying, "I see one-third of a nation ill-housed, ill-clad, ill-nourished. It is not in despair that I paint you that picture. I paint it for you in hope—because the nation, seeing and understanding the injustice in it, proposes to paint it out!"

The nation, however, could not "paint out" an even greater menace in other parts of the world. The Japanese had overrun Manchuria in 1931; Italy had grabbed Ethiopia in 1935, a civil war raged in Spain in 1936; and in 1938 and 1939 Adolf Hitler of Germany occupied Austria, swallowed

Czechoslovakia, and signed a non-aggression treaty with Russia. When Roosevelt warned that action must be taken to ensure the security of the United States he was branded an "alarmist" by his opponents.

In view of the non-aggression pact between Nazi Germany and Russia, the Communist party in the United States blasted Roosevelt as an imperialist warmonger and opposed all American assistance to the enemies of Germany.

In 1939, with another election due in 1940, Roosevelt asked for congressional authority to sell weapons and other war supplies to other countries on a cash-and-carry basis. He also requested passage of a law to enlarge the United States armed forces by conscription, or draft.

These requests split the voting public into two camps—one anxious to keep hands off in European affairs, the other supporting the President.

The big question was whether or not Franklin Roosevelt would shatter tradition by running for a third term. Early in 1940 he considered issuing a statement that he would not seek re-election, but before mid-year the Nazi war machine had goose-stepped into Belgium, Holland and France, and the threat of another world war was very real. The Democrats pleaded with Roosevelt to run again, partly because of the war threat and partly because they had no other candidate who could match his powers as a vote-getter.

Roosevelt shattered precedent by accepting the Democratic nomination on the grounds that it was his patriotic duty to do so.

His Republican opponent was Wendell Willkie, a wealthy New York attorney and utilities magnate, who campaigned in rumpled clothes and tousled hair on a platform of keeping out of war. The Democrats called him "the barefoot boy from

THE BIG SLUMP, THE NEW DEAL AND "IKE" 155

Wall Street." The Republicans tried to pound home a warning that Roosevelt's re-election would mean a dictatorship for America and the vanishing of free choice.

While Willkie rushed tirelessly from city to city making political speeches and pleading for support, Roosevelt stayed close to the White House and declared that the international and domestic problems were so vital that they demanded his attention more than did a political campaign. If the people wanted him they would say so at the polls, and he would serve.

The people did want him, and he carried thirty-eight states to Willkie's ten. For the first time in its history the United States had elected a President for a third term.

In 1941 almost all of Europe was caught up in the war. The Nazis had torn up the non-aggression treaty with the Soviets and had invaded Russia without warning. Promptly the Communist party in the United States did an about-face and urged America to help her Russian "friend."

On December 7, 1941, the Japanese bombed Pearl Harbor, inflicting terrific damage to the American Pacific battle fleet, and the United States was in a fight to the finish.

By 1944 there were good prospects for an Allied victory, and the Democrats wanted Roosevelt to try for a fourth term —a proposal heretofore undreamed of even in the most imaginative of political minds. Roosevelt said that he would accept the nomination if it were offered, and that he would serve if he were elected. He was nominated, along with Senator Harry S. Truman of Missouri as the Vice Presidential candidate.

Their Republican counterparts were Governor Thomas E. Dewey of New York and Governor John W. Bricker of Ohio. Dewey, who had won a reputation as a prosecuting "racket buster" in New York, was generally conceded to be a shrewd and brilliant politician whose vote-getting powers must not be underrated.

When the vote avalanche was counted in November, Roosevelt had been elected for the fourth time.

In February, 1945, Roosevelt met the Russian leader, Joseph Stalin, and the British Prime Minister, Sir Winston Churchill, at Yalta, to talk about the peace that would follow the victory now in sight. When he returned to the United States he was gaunt, tired and ill, and on April 12 he collapsed and died suddenly at Warm Springs, Georgia.

On that evening Harry S. Truman was sworn in at the White House as President of the United States.

Mr. Truman had been a farmer, a haberdasher and a county judge in Missouri, later won an election as a senator from that state. Shortly after he took office as President, forty-six countries joined in an historic conference in San Francisco, and the United Nations came into being. One participant was the United States, whose membership recalled the 1919 dream of Woodrow Wilson for a League of Nations.

Before April ended, the Italian dictator, Benito Mussolini, had been killed by his own countrymen, the Allies had occupied Berlin, and Adolf Hitler had committed suicide. During the first week in May, Germany surrendered.

The war in the Pacific continued. President Truman flew the Atlantic in July to talk with Stalin and Churchill, and in August he made one of the most fateful decisions in his career or that of any President. He authorized the use of the world's first atomic bomb against Japan, and on August 6 this terrible weapon, carried and released by a single United States aircraft, utterly destroyed the city of Hiroshima. A second atom bomb decimated Nagasaki only three days later, and the Japa-

THE BIG SLUMP, THE NEW DEAL AND "IKE"   157

nese then surrendered unconditionally. World War II was over.

In 1948 many Democrats expected that Truman would be their nominee, but others thought they might have a better chance of winning with General Dwight D. Eisenhower, who was fresh in the public mind as a war hero. Eisenhower refused to accept the nomination if it were offered, on the grounds that the "subordination of the military to civil power will be best sustained when lifelong professional soldiers abstain from seeking high political office." He was a "lifelong professional soldier."

It was at this time that the United States prepared to join other free nations in a "North Atlantic Treaty Organization" (NATO), under which they would stand together in armed defense against Communist aggression. Henry Wallace, a former Vice President of the United States, argued that the American policy of "get tough with Russia" would bring about another war. He organized a "Progressive movement" in which he became the Presidential candidate of a new political group, the "Progressive" party, with Senator Glen H. Taylor of Idaho as his teammate. This party had the backing of the Communists.

Because President Truman took a strong stand in favor of civil rights legislation, a southern segment of his own Democratic party refused to support him. Instead, this "Dixiecrat" group formed a new "States' Right" party with Governor J. Strom Thurmond of South Carolina for President. By this move the southern bloc hoped to divert enough votes to force the election into the House of Representatives.

The Republican team was New York's Governor Thomas E. Dewey for President and California's Governor Earl Warren for the second place.

Once the race was on, a strange thing happened. Both the Republicans and the Democrats believed that Truman would be defeated. Political columnists predicted a Dewey victory. Public-opinion polls showed that Dewey's election was practically assured. One man, however, ignored the predictions and the polls. He was Harry Truman, and he criss-crossed the country with his wife and daughter to meet thousands of voters, ridiculing the "do-nothing" Republican Congress and outlining his "Fair Deal" program for continued progress.

On election night Governor Dewey (like Charles Evans Hughes thirty-two years earlier) was feeling like a President-elect. In some metropolitan cities, such as Chicago, early editions of newspapers carried banner headlines announcing Dewey's victory even before the votes were counted. Amid all the hullaballoo and while returns were still coming in, Harry Truman went to bed. When he rose in the morning he found that he had won the election—just as he had expected!

By this time the United States was already engaged in a "cold war" with Russia, and in his inaugural address President Truman proposed a four-point program for fighting Communism by giving technical aid to underdeveloped countries.

Communism was on the march with a vengeance. On June 25, 1950, armies of the "Communist People's Republic" of North Korea, equipped with Russian armor, aircraft and weapons, stormed across the thirty-eighth parallel into the Republic of South Korea. Promptly the United States asked the United Nations to condemn the attack and require the Communists to withdraw from non-Communist South Korea.

While the question was still under debate in the United Nations, President Truman rushed American troops to fight on the side of the South Koreans in what he called "a police action." Subsequently United Nations forces joined in the anti-Communist fight.

In 1951 the states ratified the Twenty-second Amendment to the Constitution, which limits the President to a maximum of two successive terms in office. When Franklin Roosevelt announced during his second term that he was available for a third, his dealings with statesmen abroad and his plans and promises for new policies at home took on force and power that might have been lacking if it were certain that he must leave the White House when his second term expired. Today a President who serves one term and is re-elected becomes a "lame duck," and since it is certain that he cannot serve a third term, many believe that his political power weakens accordingly.

As the Korean war dragged on and on, several people were arrested in the United States for selling stolen atomic secrets to the Russians. Investigations of Communists in government, which Truman had earlier belittled as "red herring" investigations, attracted wide attention, partly through wild and often unfounded charges made by Republican Senator Joseph R. McCarthy of Wisconsin. In several instances, however, the investigations did turn up enemy agents, and Mr. Truman's term "red herring" was used by Republicans to criticize him for his failure to recognize the dangers of the Communist conspiracy within the government.

By 1952, when another election was in preparation, the Korean "police action" was stalemated, months of truce talks with the Communists were getting nowhere, Congressional investigations had revealed evidences of bribery and other offenses in the Internal Revenue Bureau and the Justice Department's Tax Division, and the popularity of Truman and the Democratic party was fading fast.

The chances for a Republican victory were good if the right candidate could be found. Senator Robert A. Taft of Ohio was a prospect, but he was an isolationist who had opposed Truman's policy of helping underdeveloped foreign countries, and this was now considered outmoded thinking. As an alternative the Republicans turned to General Dwight D. ("Ike") Eisenhower, who was then commander of the North Atlantic Treaty Organization.

Eisenhower, like Grant before him, was strictly a military figure with no political experience. Shortly before the United States entered World War II he was promoted from a lieutenant colonel to the temporary rank of brigadier general. In 1942 he was given the temporary rank of major general and placed in command of U. S. forces in the European Theater of War. His first campaign as such was the successful invasion of North Africa, and in 1943 he became commanding general of all Allied forces in the European Theater, with instructions to plan the invasion of western Europe. One June 6, 1944, his invasion plans ("Operation Overlord") were put in motion, and the greatest amphibious military operation in world history struck the Nazis on the beaches of Normandy.

Eisenhower continued as Supreme Commander of the Allied forces until Germany surrendered unconditionally on May 8, 1945. He later became Chief of Staff, but retired on May 2, 1948, to accept a post as President of Columbia University. It was on December 19, 1950, that he was recalled to military duty as Supreme Commander of NATO.

As with Zachary Taylor in 1847, no one knew definitely what Eisenhower's political leanings were. At one time President Truman had offered to help him win the Democratic nomination if he wanted it, but Eisenhower indicated that he was not interested nor was he equipped to become President.

THE BIG SLUMP, THE NEW DEAL AND "IKE"

His statement that he wanted nothing to do with politics had a familiar historical echo. General Grant, an earlier candidate, said, "I am a soldier—not a statesman." General Zach Taylor in 1846 declared, "For the office of President I have no aspiration whatever." Both Grant and Taylor became Presidents.

In 1952 General Eisenhower likewise was induced to resign his command and become the Republican candidate. The Vice Presidential runner was Senator Richard M. Nixon of California.

The Democratic standard bearers were Governor Adlai E. Stevenson of Illinois and Senator John J. Sparkman of Alabama, the latter chosen in an effort to heal the breach with the South and bring the rebellious "Dixiecrats" back into the fold.

In this campaign, television played a vital role. In earlier days the voters formed opinions by seeing and hearing candidates in person, or by reading about them in newspapers and magazines. When radio was introduced, millions of people at home listened to millions of broadcast words. With the advent and growth of television, families now sat in living rooms and saw and heard the candidates as they made their campaign promises.

A well-known television personality, Jackie Gleason, once said, "If you believed everything the candidates said, you wouldn't vote for either one of them!" His point was that each belabored the other so viciously that neither would seem competent to direct the affairs of the nation.

Television helped to get Senator Nixon out of a tough spot. While Eisenhower and the Republicans preached purity and condemned the Democratic "mess in Washington," a New York newspaper startled them with a story that Nixon had accepted some $18,000 from friends and supporters in California to help pay expenses in his campaign. The Democrats called him "Tricky Dicky," and there was fast talk among Republicans about having Nixon resign as the Vice Presidential candidate.

Finally Mr. Nixon made an impressive appeal on a special nationwide television program, declaring that he had received no personal benefit from the money and had used it only to do a better job. He made sentimental references to his "little dog, Checkers," and to his wife's "cloth coat," thus contrasting her clothing with mink coats which had allegedly been accepted as gifts by prominent Democrats. The TV program had been prepared under the direction of the best professional publicists the Republicans could hire, and it paid off, for Nixon was not only retained but also won the support of many undecided voters.

General Eisenhower, in his campaign, also won a host of votes by making a statement that said little but implied much. "If elected," he said, "I shall go to Korea." The implication was that he could bring the drawn-out Korean war to a quick finish. People associated Eisenhower with the winning of World War II and looked upon him as a hero and a kind of fatherly symbol of security, all of which added up to his election as President in 1952.

Mr. Eisenhower seemed deeply resentful of critical remarks made against him and the Republicans by Harry Truman during the Presidential race. To Mr. Truman, however, all word-whippings in a political campaign were merely part of the game, with no personal malice intended. When President Truman invited President-elect Eisenhower to breakfast at the White House, Mr. Eisenhower declined the invitation; and on Inauguration Day when Eisenhower arrived at the

White House to join Truman for the traditional parade to the Capitol, "Ike" refused to leave his car and waited for Truman to come out—a most discourteous gesture. To a degree it was history over again—Andrew Jackson had refused to call on his predecessor, John Quincy Adams, and the incoming U. S. Grant and outgoing Andrew Johnson had refused to join each other for the inaugural.

CHAPTER

11

THE COMING OF THE NEW FRONTIER

November 12, 1956: Mr. Eisenhower has been re-elected on the Republican ticket. There is an armistice in Korea, but we are having troubles at home, one of them involves civil rights. More bluntly, it has to do with recognizing the Negro as a first-class, not second-class, American citizen and giving him the privileges and rights due all Americans. In 1954 the Supreme Court ordered the end of all "separate-but-equal" facilities for Negroes. Since that time there have been clashes between the integrationists and the segregationists, and they may get worse before they get better.

Election Day, 1960: For the first time in our history a Roman Catholic has been elected President. He is John Fitzgerald Kennedy of Boston, a Democrat, and the strange fact is that the voters chose him over his Republican opponent, Richard Nixon, at a time when the nation was enjoying peace and prosperity under a Republican administration. Most people agree that a series of television debates between Nixon and Kennedy helped to swing a host of undecided votes to Kennedy, which indicates how important electronics have become in our daily lives. Young John Kennedy will have a difficult task, for the whole world is in turmoil and the President of the United States faces one of the most crucial periods in our history. As he himself has said, "It isn't 'What can my country do for me?'—it's 'What can I do for my country?'" This is the question we must all ask ourselves.

JUST as he promised, Mr. Eisenhower did go to Korea soon after his election and found simply that armistice negotiations, which had been going on for more than two years, were on the verge of completion, except for a question about exchanging prisoners. This was settled a few months later and an uneasy truce was signed July 27, 1953. But the thirty-eighth parallel was still the dividing line between free and Communist Korea.

A dividing line of another kind created trouble in 1954, when the U. S. Supreme Court handed down a decision that "separate-but-equal" facilities for Negroes must end because such conditions violated the Fourteenth Amendment to the Constitution. This meant, among other things, that Negroes could no longer be lawfully segregated in schools or public places, as was the practice in several states. Immediately various organizations, such as the National Association for the Advancement of Colored People (NAACP), began to make "test" cases by sending Negroes into hitherto segregated areas, resulting in fist fights and near-riots.

On top of President Eisenhower's many political and social problems he was plunged into a fight for life itself in September, 1955, when he suffered a severe heart attack in Denver, Colorado. Within two months, however, he was back in Washington, and early in 1956 he announced that he was available for another Presidential term.

Once again the "father image," the wide smile, the magnetic personality brought out enough "I Like Ike" voters to keep Eisenhower in the White House. As in the cases of Herbert Hoover and Martin Van Buren, the nation seemed to be doing well as this term began. Then in 1957 came a business "recession" which burdened towns and cities, and five to six million people were unemployed.

The Supreme Court's decision on integration had fomented racial clashes in many places. In Little Rock, Arkansas, Governor Orval Faubus defied the Court in 1957 and ordered the Arkansas National Guard to see that no Negro children entered Central High School. When Faubus also ignored a court order obtained by the NAACP requiring him to open the school to Negroes, President Eisenhower sent armed paratroopers into Little Rock to see that the court order was obeyed. Thus the ghosts of the Reconstruction period were haunting Little Rock and other American cities.

The President was also seriously disturbed about another problem in his own official family, a problem such as had beset Grant and Harding. A congressional committee revealed that a Boston industrial tycoon named Bernard Goldfine had received "favors" after presenting expensive gifts to Sherman Adams, former governor of New Hampshire, who was Eisenhower's "strong right arm" and White House chief of staff. Adams, it appeared, was an old friend of Goldfine's and had interceded for him with certain government agencies with which Goldfine had business dealings.

Although any wrongdoing was vigorously denied, the Republicans insisted on Adams' dismissal because they believed that if he stayed he would hurt their election chances. The Democrats demanded it because Eisenhower had condemned the Truman administration for similar activity and had vowed that he would "clean up the mess in Washington." As the squabble raged, Mr. Adams resigned voluntarily.

A whole new era began in October, 1957, when the Russians placed the first artificial satellite (Sputnik I) in orbit around the earth. Not only was this a great scientific accomplishment, but also it served notice on the world, and especially to the United States, that Russia was leading the parade in the development of rockets and missiles—a field in which America lagged because of government economy in the national defense program. The space race had begun.

In Eisenhower's administration the entire world was being caught up in a web of tension. Besides civil rights agitation at home, there were revolts against the French in Algeria, against the British in Cyprus, a rebellion in Indonesia, border fights in Israel, bombardments of the Chinese Nationalists on Formosa by Communists from Red China, and a gathering storm over West Berlin and Communist-dominated East Berlin in Germany.

When the time came to choose candidates for the 1960 Presidential elections Mr. Eisenhower endorsed Vice President Nixon as his choice to succeed him. Nixon was the Republican nominee, with Henry Cabot Lodge of Massachusetts for the Vice Presidency.

In the Democratic ranks a young senator from Massachusetts, John Fitzgerald Kennedy, went into action with a smooth-running organization headed by his younger brother, Robert. Thanks to brilliant planning, tireless persuasion of convention delegates, and sheer hard driving, the Kennedy team bowled over the opposition and chalked up a winning score for their league. John F. Kennedy won the nomination as the Democratic candidate for the Presidency, with Senator Lyndon B. Johnson of Texas for second place.

"Jack" Kennedy was no newcomer to politics. He was the grandson of Boston politicians and the son of Joseph P. Kennedy, one-time United States Ambassador to Great Britain. Young John had served in the House of Representatives and the Senate. As a lieutenant aboard a PT boat in the Pacific in World War II he had distinguished himself in battle and emerged as a wounded hero. Now he was in another kind of fight, this time for the Presidency of the United States.

Many members of his own party doubted his ability to win. Under Eisenhower and the Republicans the country was at peace and there was a substantial degree of prosperity. Would Kennedy's youth have a special appeal, or would it be a handicap? Richard Nixon, his Republican rival, was young, too. But there was something else that might bring about a crushing defeat for John Kennedy. He was a Roman Catholic, and no Catholic had ever been elected President. The only one who had tried was Al Smith, and most people agreed that Smith's church affiliation was a major factor in his defeat.

Candidate Kennedy, however, waded boldly into the religious issue in his campaign, declaring that he was strongly in favor of the separation of church and state. A man's religion should not influence a voter's decision, yet in 1960 there were echoes of the Al Smith whispering campaign and they were publicly condemned by campaigners on both sides, including Mr. Nixon.

Mr. Nixon, recalling the favorable effect of Mr. Eisenhower's campaign promise, "I shall go to Korea," decided to use the same bit with a slight change. The most troublesome of international relationships was that between the United States and the Soviet Union, and although the Russo-American situation had been tense and strained while Mr. Nixon was Vice President, he now declared, "If elected, I will go to Russia."

The country reached a new pitch of election excitement when it was announced that Kennedy and Nixon were to engage in a series of television debates. Here was a reflection of the Lincoln–Douglas oratorical contest, with one tremendous difference. Lincoln and Douglas had debated before "live" audiences of several thousand people, and without benefit of amplifiers or other electronic equipment. Kennedy and Nixon would meet in quiet studios and talk into cameras and microphones that would carry their pictures and voices to 120 million or more people.

Before the series began, Nixon was a much more familiar public figure than Kennedy, who had proposed the TV appearances. It is likely that Nixon and his advisers believed the debates would stamp him as a mature, wise and competent statesman, showing up Kennedy as a boyish freshman in the hard school of big-time politics.

Kennedy, however, projected into millions of homes a fresh and vigorous personality that inspired confidence, and demonstrated by quick thought and intelligent argument that he was entirely capable of fulfilling the obligations of the Presidency.

In the debates and throughout his campaign Kennedy kept hammering at the theme that America's peace and prosperity were uneasy and endangered; that the Republican foreign policy, defense policy and economic policy were so weak and shaky that the United States had lost prestige in other countries and was threatened by a modern sword of Damocles hanging by a Communist thread.

When the TV series ended, Kennedy's face and voice were as familiar to Americans as a map of the United States, and any doubts as to his maturity and political competence were swept away. Also, many undecided voters were won over to the Kennedy cause.

Thousands of other voters would support *neither* Kennedy nor Nixon, but would instead stand firm as members of third or minor parties whose aims differed from those of the Democrats and Republicans.

For example, the "American Beat Consensus" nominated a Chicago bookseller named William Lloyd Smith as its Presidential candidate. The party consisted primarily of non-conformists (beatniks) whose non-conforming platform was

Dreamsville, dad, like way out. Samples: "Abolish the working class. Provide a ten-billion-dollar subsidy for artists. Forget the budget, just balance the debt. Make peace with everybody, because all beatniks are cowards. Legalize nepotism, favoritism, excess profits and mink coats."

Oldest of the minor contestants was the Prohibition party, which had entered every Presidential race since 1872. Its perennial goal of doing away with alcoholic drinks was only one of many planks in its 1960 platform. Others plugged for world peace, reforms in marriage and divorce laws, opposition to Communism and to government extravagance. Its Presidential candidate was Dr. Rutherford L. Decker, Pastor of the Temple Baptist Church in Kansas City, Missouri.

The Socialist party, one of the better-known minor groups, decided (for the first time since 1900) not to nominate a candidate. Its founder, the late Eugene V. Debs, had campaigned and lost in five elections, and his successor, Norman Thomas, failed in six. Thomas's successor, Darlington Hoopes, polled only 2126 votes in the 1956 election, and this poor showing probably motivated the party's withdrawal in 1960.

Poor showings have no discouraging effect on some candidates. Henry Krajewski, a tavern owner and former pig farmer from Secaucus, New Jersey, ran for the Presidency in 1952, 1956 and 1960 as the candidate of the "Poor Man's" party. He advocated free beer for everybody and a lowered income tax. In some of his public appearances in 1960 he carried a squealing pig under one arm as a "symbol of peace and prosperity." Explanation: The pig is a peaceful creature; and when he's butchered, every part of the carcass, from pork chops to pig's ear, is usable. As Candidate Krajewski asked, "Who wants to eat donkey or elephant?"

The Socialist Labor party candidate was Eric Hass, publisher of his party's newspaper, who drew more than 41,000 votes in 1956. The party urged government control of industry, abolition of capitalism, and the adoption of socialism as outlined by Karl Marx.

The Socialist Worker's party, subscribing to the philosophies of Leon Trotsky, nominated Farrell Dobbs of New York as its candidate. This former truck driver netted some 5500 votes in the 1956 Presidential race. The party's aims in 1960 included destruction of all American nuclear weapon stockpiles, withdrawal of all United States military forces from foreign soil, and the establishment of a socialistic society.

Notably missing among the minors was the Communist Party of the United States, whose major objective was the forceful overthrow of the American government. Early in 1962, as this book was written, the Communist party was facing federal prosecution and was believed preparing to "go underground." Under a 1950 federal law (the Internal Security Act) the members and officials of the party were required to register as agents of the Soviet Union. The Communists fought the law in the courts, but in 1961 it was upheld by the Supreme Court, and when party chiefs and members failed to register by a specified deadline, the party was indicted by a federal grand jury. At this writing, further action by the Department of Justice is pending.

Voters who preferred a potato instead of a chicken in every pot could support Symon Gould of New York, candidate of the Vegetarian party, whose program was simple and understandable: Abolish atomic war as "a contemplated cannibalistic sacrifice of youth"; and peace and plenty for all, in a meatless society.

In Chicago the "America First" party candidate, Lar Daly, attracted considerable attention for two reasons: He made his campaign speeches while wearing an "Uncle Sam" suit—top hat, cutaway coat, striped trousers, stars and all. More than that, however, he clamored constantly for radio and television stations to give or sell minor party candidates "equal time" to that utilized by the major parties for political messages.

Mr. Daly's one-man crusade was a prime factor in bringing about a congressional action to suspend the "equal time" provisions for the 1960 campaign in order to make possible the Kennedy–Nixon television debates.

In Los Angeles, California, in February, 1960, a movement was launched to nominate Governor Orval Faubus of Arkansas for the Presidency, on the grounds that Faubus was "the man to lead this country back to God's way." Later a "National States' Rights" party was organized in Florida, with Faubus as its Presidential candidate and a platform dedicated to white supremacy.

One candidate without a party was reported to be expecting considerable help from "space men." Gabriel Green of Whittier, California, declared that he had not only seen scores of flying saucers but also had actually talked with visitors from outer space. He was sure he could poll several million votes, based upon helpful information to be provided by his friends from other worlds.

More down-to-earth was the Texas Constitution party, with its thirty-five-year-old candidate, Charles L. Sullivan of Clarksdale, Mississippi. Members of this group described themselves as "Jeffersonian Democrats" and stood for "Constitutional conservatism," claiming that the election of the Republican or Democratic candidates would represent the "final defeat from which Constitutional liberty cannot expect to recover." It was the hope of this party that its followers, joining similar groups in several states, could siphon off enough votes to prevent either of the major candidates from getting a majority, in which event the election would have to be decided in the House of Representatives.

The Constitution figured in the program of still another group—the Constitution party, whose nominee was Merritt B. Curtis of Washington, D. C. Among the party's platform planks was one to abolish income taxes and one advocating American withdrawal from the United Nations.

On October 30, only a few days before voters would go to the polls, the Columbia Broadcasting System set aside one hour of free television time and invited candidates of the minor political parties to appear in a TV program called "Other Hats in the Ring."

When Eric Hass, the Socialist Labor candidate, arrived at the CBS studios he learned that some minor parties had not accepted the invitation and that only the Prohibition party, the Vegetarian party and the American Beat party were to appear with him. Thereupon he refused to participate on the grounds that the program was a "farcical flea circus," and that it would not dignify him or his party to appear with the Vegetarian and Beatnik candidates.

Two other minor parties were active in 1960 to promote the interests of Negroes and to find solutions to racial problems in the United States. One, the Independent Afro-American party, nominated Dr. Martin Luther King as its candidate. The other, the Afro-American party, was led by the Reverend Clennon King of Albany, Georgia.

One of the least aggressive of all minor party candidates was Mr. Connie N. Watts of Banks County, Georgia. Mr. Watts made no whirlwind trips, no whistle-stop speeches, no spectacular charges or promises. For the most part his headquarters were in a rocking chair on the front porch of his home; and if elected, one of his brightest hopes was to sponsor the passage of "a law to keep them 'vine-ripened' stickers off of them mushy green tomatoes."

Mr. Watts and other lesser-known candidates for the Presidency often face one major obstacle—getting their names on the ballot. Various states require political groups to meet certain requirements before they can be listed on a ballot. Generally this can be done if the party has polled a specified number of votes in a previous election or if the party submits a petition bearing a specified number of signatures. New York State, for example, requires at least 12,000 names on such a petition, but the number varies in other states.

In the absence of a party name on the ballot, voters may "write in" the name of any person for whom they want to vote. In such cases, however, the votes are for *electors*, not for the candidates named. A "write in" vote for Connie Watts, for example, would count as one vote for Mr. Watts as a Presidential elector, not as a direct vote for Mr. Watts.

Although many minor parties never expect to win a Presidential election, their very existence is important because they prove that we are a free people in a free country, privileged to speak our minds, to disagree with our government's actions and policies, and to cast a ballot for an obscure or little-known American citizen who aspires to be President of the United States. This is Democracy in action.

Actually the Republican party of today began as a "third party," a coalition of Whigs, Democrats and Free Soilers, which points up the possibility that under certain circumstances a minor may become a major party.

Of much greater significance is the fact that many of the ideas and proposals set out by minor parties in the past, including the income tax, Social Security, unemployment insurance, federal highway programs, and other progressive movements, were subsequently adopted by the major parties as being in the best interests of the nation.

In the 1960 election the country was almost evenly divided between candidates Nixon and Kennedy, but the big cities and the powerful southern bloc helped swing the balance to Kennedy, who thus became the first Roman Catholic President in United States history, in one of the closest elections of modern times. Many political analysts were convinced that Mr. Kennedy's performances in the unprecedented television debates were a major factor in his victory.

The new President didn't live to finish his first term. He was shot and killed by Lee Harvey Oswald on November 22, 1963, in Dallas, Texas.

Within hours, Vice President Lyndon Baines Johnson was sworn in as President. His most explosive political inheritance was the war in Vietnam. The few military "advisors" first sent to South Vietnam by President Eisenhower had boomed into a major military force under President Kennedy. Mr. Johnson increased it to about half a million American troops.

In domestic battles, black people rebelled against poverty and widespread racial injustice. The Reverend Martin Luther King, Jr., a respected black leader who sought justice without violence, was shot and killed in Memphis, Tennessee, in 1968. In Washington, Los Angeles and other cities there were violent clashes in which rioters and policemen were killed and wounded. Stores were looted and burned by militants on the rampage.

Angry young people, white and black, stormed colleges and demanded a greater voice in administration and curricula. Vandalism was rampant.

Crime skyrocketed in cities. Officials blamed its growth on

the widening use of dangerous drugs and on poverty, environment and lack of education.

Youth adopted new styles in dress, hair, and living. Boys and girls welcomed the new "sexual freedom." Nudity on stage and screen was common. Adults once shockable were becoming shockproof, but critical.

In rebuttal, youth ridiculed the hypocrisy of adult alcoholism and undercover sex. They also showed how outmoded were many educational methods and curricula of the new age.

Some of these conditions had faced President Johnson in 1964 when he defeated Republican Senator Barry Goldwater. The new Vice President was former Senator Hubert H. Humphrey of Minnesota.

Mr. Johnson envisioned a "Great Society" in which all Americans could live in peace and reasonable prosperity. His administration did make important strides in civil rights, voting rights, and antipoverty measures, but found no easy solutions to problems of wars, decay in the cities, racism, pollution, inflation, and all the other hazards of modern American life. These were some of the issues in the 1968 political campaigns.

The 1968 campaigns were marked by surprises. With Mr. Johnson expected to seek reelection as the Democratic nominee, Democratic Senator Eugene McCarthy of Minnesota announced his candidacy. Thousands of young people rallied to his "peace platform," pleading with voters to sweep clean with Gene.

From the South came George Wallace, former governor of Alabama, as leader of the American Independent Party. Mr. Wallace ridiculed the "eggheads" in Washington, blasted the militants, advocated an American military victory in Vietnam, and called for the arrests of pro-Vietcong demonstrators as traitors to the United States.

National tension was building up. Suddenly and unexpectedly, President Johnson announced that he would order limited bombing in Vietnam and that he would not seek reelection. Many considered the decision a sacrifice to show that his efforts for a negotiated settlement had no political motivation.

After Mr. Johnson's withdrawal, and after Senator McCarthy won a major victory in the New Hampshire primary, Senator Robert Kennedy stepped into the Presidential contest.

So did Vice President Hubert Humphrey.

So did Senator George McGovern of South Dakota.

All four were after the Democratic nomination.

The Republican front-runner was Richard Milhouse Nixon, who had served as Vice President in the Eisenhower administration. Mr. Nixon had been defeated by John F. Kennedy in the 1960 Presidential election.

In the midst of the campaigns another tragedy saddened the nation. After making a political talk in a Los Angeles hotel, Senator Robert Kennedy was shot and killed by a Jordanian, Sirhan Sirhan, apparently because the assassin considered Kennedy a friend of Israel and an enemy of the Arabs.

The Republican convention in Miami Beach, Florida, chose Mr. Nixon as its candidate. His rivals had been Governors Nelson A. Rockefeller of New York and Ronald Reagan of California.

The Democrats, in Chicago, nominated Mr. Humphrey.

In a close election, Richard Nixon became the new President. His Vice President was Spiro T. Agnew, former governor of Maryland. Mr. Nixon thanked the "forgotten man"—the middle-aged, middle-class "silent majority"—for contributing to his victory.

Political analysts said the Republican triumph was due

largely to the fact that the Democratic Party was split by too much fighting within its own ranks. This view was supported by elections of Republican governors and mayors in various states and cities, some of which were upsets.

In Virginia, for instance, where the well-known "Byrd machine" had long ruled the political roost, voters in 1969 elected Linwood Holton to be the state's first Republican governor in this century.

The Republicans gained four other governships, for a total of 31 in the 50 states. They also increased their power in the Senate and House of Representatives, although Democrats held control of both houses.

In New York City, Mayor John Lindsay was reelected after many prophets predicted his defeat.

Carl Stokes, Negro Republican mayor of Cleveland, Ohio, also won out against stiff opposition.

Experts tried in vain to explain happenings on the political front. Some said that Americans were fed up with policing the world and were demanding more action on domestic problems. Some believed that voters hoped the Republicans could combat violence, strikes, crime, poverty and drugs more effectively than the Democrats who had been in power for so many years. Others pointed out that George Wallace had received almost a whopping 10 million votes for the Presidency, and that Republican promises approached those of Wallace closely enough to warrant a Republican swing by numerous Wallace supporters.

Whatever the political situation, the United States must continue to seek answers to questions about air and water pollution, the drug traffic, crime, civil rights, housing, poverty, disarmament, trade, foreign policy and entanglements, inflation, education, transportation and other important problems that plague our nation.

If the government's solutions to these and other problems do not satisfy us, then we, the American people, can change our leadership by our votes, for this is the essence of a Constitutional democracy. Strangely enough, it is often the political party *not* in power which, by its opposition, its criticisms and recommendations, creates guide lines which the reigning party feels impelled to follow, and this is one of the advantages of our two-party system.

We, the people, are supposed to govern ourselves—but do we? Few of us take the trouble to learn what our representative or senator said in Congress (or in our state legislature) today or this week, or whether he voted, or how, or upon what. But we ought to know, because he or she is supposed to be saying and doing what we want said and done, and the laws he helps to pass affect all of us in one way or another.

Of course if our representative or senator doesn't *know* what we want or what we think about matters that concern us, he can't very well express our wishes, so he does the next best thing and follows his own best judgment or the line of his political party and its leaders, teaming up with his colleagues who also get little or no guidance from their constituents. He becomes more and more a representative of the party and less and less a representative of the people.

You and I and millions of other Americans can decide what we want our politicians to do or not to do—but a decision without some action is as useless as an automobile without an engine.

Your opinion and that of your next-door neighbor on a single subject may be exactly opposite, but we ought to express those opinions and let our lawmakers be governed by the wishes of the majority. That's what makes democracy, and making democracy is the most important production job in the world today.

We Americans have power as individuals because we have a vote. But how do we use it? Do we vote for a President, a governor, a mayor, or a town councilman because he is handsome? Or fatherly? Or likable? Or a good speaker? Or do we first learn just what he stands for and how his plans and beliefs will affect our nation and our lives?

Votes are vital in the career of a member of Congress. He pleads for them, makes promises for them, and if he gets enough of them, he becomes a duly elected servant of the people. Most people who hire servants tell them what to do and see if they do it. The House of Representatives and the Senate—and the houses of the state legislatures—are our houses. Their members are our hired servants. Are they doing the kind of job that suits us, or are they wondering just what it is we want done?

What are your orders for today? What entries will you make in *your* Diary of Democracy?

SUGGESTED FURTHER READING

A Short History of American Democracy, by John D. Hicks and George E. Mowry. Houghton Mifflin, Boston, 1956.
American Nation, The, by John D. Hicks. Houghton Mifflin, Boston, 1955.
American Party System, The, by Charles E. Merriam and Harold M. Gosnell. Macmillan, New York, 1949.
American Political and Social History, by Harold U. Faulkner. Appleton–Century–Crofts, New York, 1952.
American Political Parties, by Wilfrid E. Binkley. Knopf, New York, 1958.
American Politics and the Party System, by Hugh A. Bone. McGraw-Hill, New York, 1955.
An Almanac of Liberty, by William O. Douglas. Doubleday, Garden City, N. Y., 1954.
Century of Struggle, by Eleanor Flexner. Harvard University Press, Cambridge, Mass., 1959.
Communist Party of the United States of America, The. Senate Document No. 117, 84th Congress, 2d Session. Government Printing Office, Washington 25, D. C., 1956.
Democracy in America, by Alexis deTocqueville. Knopf, New York, 1945.
Dictionary of American Politics, edited by Edward C. Smith and Arnold J. Zurcher. Barnes & Noble, New York, 1955.
The Farther Shores of Politics, by George Thayer. Simon & Schuster, New York, 1967.
Federal Union, The, by John D. Hicks. Houghton Mifflin, Boston, 1957.
The Limits of Power, by Eugene McCarthy. Holt, Rinehart & Winston, New York, 1967.

SUGGESTED FURTHER READING

Making of the President 1960, The, by Theodore H. White. Atheneum, New York, 1961.

Making of the President 1964, The, by Theodore H. White. Atheneum, New York, 1965.

Making of the President 1968, The, by Theodore H. White. Atheneum, New York, 1969.

Manner of Selecting Delegates to National Political Conventions and the Nomination and Election of Presidential Electors. Compiled by Senate Library. Government Printing Office, Washington 25, D. C. No. 93326, 1952.

National Party Platforms, compiled by Kirk H. Porter and Donald Bruce Johnson. University of Illinois Press, Urbana, Ill., 1961.

Opinionmakers, The, by William L. Rivers. Beacon Press, Boston, 1965.

Parties and Politics in America, by Clinton Rossiter. Cornell University Press, Ithaca, 1964.

Politics in America, by D. W. Brogan. Harper, New York, 1954.

Politics in the United States, by Henry A. Turner. McGraw-Hill, New York, 1955.

Politics, Parties and Pressure Groups, by V. O. Key, Jr. Crowell, New York, 1952.

Presidential Power, The Politics of Leadership, by Richard E. Neustadt. John Wiley & Sons, New York, 1960.

Selling of the President 1968, by Joe McGinniss. Trident, New York, 1969.

To Seek A Newer World, by Robert F. Kennedy. Doubleday, Garden City, N. Y. 1969.

Third Parties in American Politics, by Howard P. Nash, Jr. Public Affairs Press, Washington, 1959.

We Elect A President, by David E. Weingast. Messner, New York, 1968.

When Presidents Meet the Press, by M. L. Stein. Messner, New York, 1969.

Where Do We Go From Here, by Martin Luther King, Jr. Harper & Row, New York, 1967.

INDEX

Adams, Charles Francis, 82
Adams, John, 21, 29, 35, 37-38, 40-42, 44
Adams, John Quincy, 54-55, 57, 60, 71, 108, 163
Adams, Samuel, 27
Adams, Sherman, 166
Afro-American party, 173
Agnew, Spiro T., 177
Agriculture, Department of, 103
Alien and Sedition Laws, 37, 39-42, 45
Allen, William "Petticoat," 75-76
American First party, 171-72
American and Foreign Christian Union, 83
American Beat Consensus, 169-70, 173
American Federation of Labor, 148
American government, purpose of, 26
American party, 89
American Political Science Association, 6
American Protestant Society, 83-84
American Railway Union, 127
American Republican party, 70, 78-79
American Woman Suffrage Association, 106, 121
Anderson, Elbert, 50-51
Anthony, Susan Brownell, 88, 105-06, 121
Anti-Catholicism, 70, 149. *See also* Native American party
Anti-Federalists, 21, 27, 33
Anti-Masonic party, 50, 57, 60-61, 63, 66

Anti-Monopoly parties, 108, 119
Anti-Saloon League, 137
Arkansas National Guard, 166
"Army of the Commonweal of Christ," 123
Arthur, Chester A., 118-19
Articles of Confederation, 19, 22, 24-25
Assassination of Andrew Jackson, attempted, 65-66
Assumption of states' debts, 31-32
Atomic bomb, first, 156
Atomic secrets, stolen, 159

Bailey, Frederick August Washington, 106
Baldwin, Luther, 40
Bank, central, 32-33, 66-67
Bank of the United States, 33, 51
Banks, state-chartered, 67, 71
"Barefoot boy from Wall Street," 154-55
Barnburners, 70, 81-82
"Bathtub gin," 140
Beecher, Henry Ward, 106
Beecher, Lyman, 87
Bell, John, 97
Bell and Everett party, 97
"Bible commonwealth," 12
Birney, James G., 71, 76-77
Black, James, 107
Blackstone Hotel, 143
Blaine, James G., 116-20
Bloomer, Amelia Jenks, 82-83, 86, 88
"Bonus march" of 1930, 150
Borah, William, 139
"Boss" Tweed, 113-15
Boston Harbor, tea dumped into, 16

INDEX

Boston Port Bill, 16
Bovay, Alvan E., 89-90
"Boy Orator of the River Platte, The," 126
"Brain Trusters," 153
Breckinridge, John C., 96
Bricker, John W., 155
"Broad Gaugers," 128
Brooks, Preston S., 92-93
Brotherhood of Locomotive Firemen, 127
Browder, Earl R., 151
Brown, B. Gratz, 107
Brutus, 16
Bryan, Charles, 147
Bryan, William Jennings, 116, 128-29, 147
Buchanan, James, 93
"Bull Moose" party, 130, 134-35
Burgesses, House of, 15, 30
Burr, Aaron, 35, 37, 41-42, 46
Butler, Andrew P., 91-92

Caesar, 16
Calhoun, John C., 37, 48, 50, 58-60, 62, 64
Capital, national, selection of location for, 31-32
Capitalism, 99, 109, 150
Carpetbaggers, 99-101, 103, 111
Cartoons, political, 51, 134. *See also* Nast, Thomas
Cary, Samuel F., 111
Cass, Lewis, 76-77, 82
Catholicism, opposition to, 77-79, 83-85
Catt, Carrie Chapman, 141
Central High School, Little Rock, 166
Chapman, Joseph, 74
Charles I, 16
Charles River, 12
"Charter" government, 13
"Checkers," 162
Christian Alliance, 83
Churchill, Sir Winston, 156
Civil rights, 157, 164
Civil Service Commission, 119
Civil War, 5, 97-98, 105, 120

Civil Works Administration, 152
Civilian Conservation Corps, 153
Clay, Henry, 37, 48, 54-55, 57-58, 63-65, 76-77, 80-81
"Clay-Adams men," 58
Cleveland, Grover, 120, 122, 127
Coffee, General, 65
"Cold war," 158
Colonial governments, types of, 13
Columbia Broadcasting System, 173
Columbia University, 18, 160
Comintern, 141
Committee of Correspondence, Virginia, 15
Common market, European, 175
Commons, House of, 15
Communism, 109, 141, 143, 145, 157-59, 165, 167, 170-71
Communist Labor party, 141
Communist party, 141, 145, 151-52, 155, 157, 171
"Communist People's Republic," 158
Communist Third International, 141
Compact, Mayflower, 11
Compromise of 1850, 86-87
"Compromiser, The Great," 55
Confederate States of America, 97
Confederation, Articles of, 19, 22, 24-25
Confederation of states, 27
"Conference for Progressive Political Action," 147-48
Congress, two-part, 26
Conkling, Roscoe, 117
"Connecticut Compromise," 26
"Conscience Whigs," 80, 82
Constitution of the United States, 21, 25-27, 32-33, 43, 45, 53, 64, 91, 96, 99, 102, 105-06, 130, 137-38, 152-53, 159, 165, 172-73
Constitution party, 173
Constitutional convention, 24-27
Constitutional Union party, 96
Continental Congress, 17-19, 30
Continental currency, value of, 22
Convention, first national political, 63
Coolidge, Calvin, 143-48
Cooper, Peter, 111

INDEX 185

Cooperatives, farm, 104
Courier and Enquirer, New York, 68
Corruption in government, 104, 107, 113-15, 117, 121, 143-44, 146-47, 159, 166
Cotton gin, Whitney's, 53
"Cotton Whigs," 80
Cox, James M., 142
Coxey, Jacob, 116, 123
"Coxey's Army," 116, 123, 150
Cranch, William, 76
Crawford, William H., 54
"Crime Against Kansas, The," 91
"Crime of '76, The," 111
Crissand, Mrs. 75
Crocker, William H., 136
Crockett, Davy, 70
Cromwell, Oliver, 14, 16
"Cross of Gold" speech, Bryan's, 126
Curtis, Merritt B., 173

Daly, Lars, 171-72
"Dark horse," first, 77
Daugherty, Harry M., 143-44
Davis, David, 107
Davis, Jefferson, 97
Davis, John W., 147
Davis, Judge, 112
Dawes, Charles G., 147
Dayton, Jonathan, 24
Debates, Lincoln-Douglas, 94-96; Kennedy-Nixon television, 164, 168-69, 172
Debs, Eugene V., 116, 127-28, 132, 137, 142-43, 170
Debtors' prisons, 22
Debts, states', assumption of, 31-32
Decker, Rutherford L., 170
Declaration of Independence, 11, 18, 20, 24, 30, 70
Declaratory Act, 16
DeLafayette, Marquis, 24
"Democratic Clubs," 34, 42
Democratic National Committee, 6
Democratic party, 50, 58, 63-64, See also Democrats
Democratic party, National, 126
"Democratic-Republicans," 42, 49-50, 53, 55, 57-58

Democrats, 58, 60, 67-69, 71, 73-77, 81-82, 86, 89-90, 96-98, 100, 103-05, 107-10, 112, 119-22, 125-26, 128, 130, 134, 136-37, 139, 142, 145, 151-59, 161-64, 167-69, 174-75, 176, 177-78
Depression, economic, in 1930s, 150
Depression of 1894, 122-23
Detroit *Tribune*, 90
Dewey, Thomas E., 155, 157-58
"Dixiecrats," 157, 161
Dobbs, Farrell, 171
Donkey, Democratic, 105
Doubleday, Abner, 97
Douglas, Stephen, 86, 88-91, 94-97
Douglass, Frederick, 106
Draft (conscription), 154
Duke of York, 13

Eaton, John H., 62
Eighteenth Amendment, 137, 140, 147, 153
Eisenhower, Dwight D., 145, 150, 157, 160-69, 175
Electoral college, 43-44, 111-12
Electoral Commission, 99, 112
Electoral procedure, 35, 37, 43-44, 54, 174
Elephant, Republican, 110-11
"Equal Rights" Amendment, 138
Equal Rights party, 67, 106
"Era of Good Feeling," 50, 52
Espionage Act, 137
Everett, Edward, 97
Executive Branch, 26

"Fair Deal," 145, 158
Farmers, 103-04, 108, 120-21, 147. *See also* Granger movement
"Father of the Constitution," 25
Faubus, Orval, 165-66, 172
Federal Emergency Relief Administration, 152
Federal Hall (New York), 28
Federal Reserve System, 135
Federalists, 21, 27, 33-35, 37-42, 46, 48-49, 52, 54-55, 93
Ferdinand Archduke Francis, 135
Fifteenth Amendment, 105-06
Fillmore, Millard, 81, 93

INDEX

"First International," 109
Foreign Evangelical Society, 83
Foreigners, influx of, 77
Fort Moultrie, 65
Fort Niagara, 56
Fort Sumter, 86, 97
Foster, William Z., 143, 152
Four-point program, Truman's, 158
Fourteenth Amendment, 105, 165
Fourth term, Roosevelt's, 155-56
France, conflict with, 19, 34, 37-39
Franklin, Benjamin, 19, 24
Free silver coinage, 122
Free Soil party, 70, 82, 86, 89-90, 174
Freemasonry, 55, 72. *See also* Anti-Masonic party
Frémont, John C., 93
French and Indian War, 15
"Front porch campaign," McKinley's, 127

"G. O. P.," 120
Garfield, James A., 116-18
Garrison, William Lloyd, 72, 91, 97
George III, 14, 16
Gerry, Elbridge, 38, 49
Gerrymander, 49
Ghent, Treaty of, 48
Gladstone, William E., 120
Gleason, Jackie, 161
Goldfine, Bernard, 166
Goldwater, Barry, 176
Gould, Symon, 171
Graft, 61
"Grand Old Party," 120
"Grange" lodges, 104
Granger movement, 99, 108. *See also* Farmers
Grant, Ulysses S., 103-04, 108, 110, 116-18, 160-61, 163, 166
Great Britain, colonial break with, 18
Great Northern Railroad, 127
Greeley, Horace, 85, 90, 107
Green, Gabriel, 172
Greenback Labor party, 116-20
Greenback party, 99, 108-09, 111, 116-17, 121
"Greenbacks," 108-09

Guadaloupe Hidalgo, Treaty of, 80
Guiteau, Charles J., 118

"Hail, Columbia!," 74
"Half-Breeds," 117
Hamilton, Alexander, 17-18, 21, 24, 27, 29-34, 41-42, 46, 53, 61
Hamlin, Hannibal, 96
Hanna, Marcus Alonzo, 116, 123-27, 129, 142
Hanna & Company, M. A., 124
"Happy Warrior, The," 148
Hard cider and log cabin campaign, 70, 73-76
Harding, Warren G., 142-45, 166
Harper's Weekly, 105
Harrison, William Henry, 47-48, 70-71, 73-76, 97, 127
Hass, Eric, 173
Haswell, Anthony, 40
Hayes, Rutherford B., 99, 111-13, 117
Hayne, Robert Y., 59
Henry, Patrick, 15-17, 27
Herald, New York, 110-11
Hermits of St. Augustine, 78
Hiroshima, 156
"His Rotundity," 37
Hitler, Adolf, 156
Hoopes, Darlington, 170
Hoover, Herbert, 142, 145, 148-53, 165
"Hooverville," 150
House of Burgesses (Virginia), 15, 30
House of Commons, 15
House of Representatives, 26, 28, 44, 54, 68, 90, 92, 102, 118, 138, 157, 167, 173, 180
Howard, Jacob M., 90
Hudson River, 28
Hughes, Charles Evans, 135-36, 158
Humphrey, Hubert H., 176, 177
Hunkers, 70, 81

Illustrations of Masonry by One of the Fraternity Who Has Devoted Thirty Years to the Subject, 56
Impeachment, attempted, of Andrew Johnson, 102

Income tax, 116, 122, 128, 170, 173-74
Independence, Declaration of, 11, 18, 20, 24, 30
Independence Hall, 21, 24
Independent Afro-American party, 173
Independent party, 108
Indiana Territory, 47-48
Indians, Tories as allies of, 18
Internal Revenue Bureau, 159
Internal Security Act, 171
International Workingmen's Association, 109
Intolerance, religious, 77-79, 83-85. *See also* Native American party
Invasion, Normandy, 160
Invisible Circle, 101

Jackson, Andrew, 49-50, 54-55, 57-58, 60-66, 68-69, 71, 76, 149, 153, 163
"Jackson men," 58
James, Duke of York, 13
Jay, John, 27
Jefferson, Thomas, 18, 21, 27, 29-37, 41-46, 53, 62, 148
"Jeffersonian Democrats," 172
"Jeffersonian Republicans," 33-35, 38-39, 44, 48, 54
"Jim Crow" laws, 103
Johnson, Andrew, 100-03, 163
Johnson, Hiram W., 134, 136, 139, 142
Johnson, Lyndon B., 167, 175-77
Judicial Branch, 26

Kansas, civil war in, 91
Kansas-Nebraska Bill, 86, 88-91, 95
Kelley, Oliver, 99, 103-04, 108
Kendall, Amos, 63
Kennedy, John Fitzgerald, 164, 167-69, 175, 176
Kennedy, Joseph P., 167
Kennedy, Robert, 167, 177
"Kentucky Resolutions," 41
King, Clennon, 173
King, Martin Luther, 173, 175
"King Andrew the First," 68
King's College (New York), 18

"Kitchen Cabinet," Jackson's, 62-63
Knapp, Isaac, 72
"Knights of the White Camellia," 101
"Know-Nothing" party, 84-85, 89, 93, 96
Knox, Reverend Hugh, 17
Korea, war in, 145, 158-59, 162, 164-65
Krajewski, Henry, 170
Ku Klux Klan, 99, 101, 103

Lafayette, Marquis De, 24
LaFollette, Robert, 147-48
"Lame ducks," 152, 159
Land, Miss Roy, 6
Lane Theological Seminary, 87
Lawrence, Richard, 66
League of Nations, 130, 138-40, 147, 156
League of Women Voters, 6, 141-42
Lee, Gideon, 67
Legislative Branch, 26
"Lenin, The American," 143
Levine, Peter, 17
Lexington, "Minute Men" at, 18
Liberal Republican party, 107-08
Liberal Republican Democratic party, 108
Liberator, The, 72
Liberty party, 70, 72, 76-77, 82
Life Among the Lowly, 87
Lincoln, Abraham, 80, 86, 94-97, 99-102
Lincoln-Douglas debates, 94-96, 168
Lindsay, John, 178
Liquor, intoxicating, opposition to, 107, 128, 137, 170
"Little Magician, The," 71
Little Rock (Arkansas), troops in, 165-66
Livingston, Robert R., 28, 45
"Locofocos," 67-68
Locomotive Firemen, Brotherhood of, 127
Lodge, Henry Cabot, 130, 139, 143, 167
"Logrolling" deal, first major, 32
Longfellow, Henry Wadsworth, 73

INDEX

Louisiana Purchase, 37, 45-46, 53, 88
Lowden, Frank O., 142
Lyon, Matthew, 40

MacArthur, Douglas, 150
Madison, James, 24-25, 27, 32, 41, 46-48, 51-52
Maine, USS, 131
Marshall John, 38
Marshall, Thomas, 140
Marx, Karl, 109, 171
Masons, 55-57. *See also* Anti-Masonic party
Massachusetts Bay Colony, 12-13, 40
Mayflower, 11-12
Mayflower Compact, 11
McCarthy, Eugene, 176, 177
McCarthy, Joseph R., 159
McKinley, William, 116, 124-32, 149
Mexico, border dispute with, 79-81
Military Hall (New York), 67
"Mill Boy of the Slashes, The," 55
Minor parties, recent, 169-74
"Minute Men," 11, 18
Missouri Compromise, 53, 88, 94
Monroe Doctrine, The, 54
Monroe, James, 45, 50, 52-54, 58
Monroe, Timothy, 56
Monticello, 30
Morgan, William, 55-56
Morris, Gouverneur, 26
Mott, Lucretia, 82, 88, 105
Mount Vernon, 22
"Mugwumps," 119-20
Mussolini, Benito, 156

Nagasaki, bombing of, 156
Napoleon, 45
"Narrow Gaugers," 128
Nast, Thomas, 105, 110, 115
National American Woman Suffrage Association, 121, 141
National Association for the Advancement of Colored People (NAACP), 165
National Democratic party, 126
National Era, 88
National Labor Reform party, 107
National Labor Union, 107

National Prohibition Act, 140
National Prohibition party, 107
National Republicans, 58, 60-61, 63, 66, 107
National States' Rights party, 172
National Temperance Society, 137
National Woman Suffrage Association, 106, 121
Native American Association, 77
Native American party, 84-85, 89
Nativism, 78-79, 149
Naturalism, unlawful, 77
Navy Department, creation of the, 39
Negroes, civil rights of, 164-66; voting by, 100
Nevis Island, B.W.I., 17
"New Deal," 145, 151, 153
New Orleans, Battle of, 49, 55, 57
New World, first political parties in the, 14
New York, Alexander Hamilton in, 17; inaugural ceremony in, 28; Stamp Act Congress in, 15
New York Times, The, 114
Nineteenth Amendment, 130, 138, 141
Nixon, Richard M., 161, 164, 167-69, 175, 177
North Atlantic Treaty Organization (NATO), 157, 160
Nullification, doctrine of, 59, 62, 64-65
"Nullification, Ordinance of," 64

O'Brien, 114
O'Conor, Charles, 108
Oberlin College, 87
Oberlin Collegiate Institute, 87
"Old Hickory," 49-50, 61, 63, 68. *See also* Jackson, Andrew
"Old Tip," 74. *See also* Harrison, William Henry
Oldham, John, 12, 40
"Operation Overlord," 160
"Order of the Sons of America, The," 84
"Order of the Star-Spangled Banner, The," 84

Oswald, Lee Harvey, 175

Palace, Hotel, 144
Pale Faces, The, 101
Panama Canal, 133
Panic of 1819, 52
Panic of 1837, 71
Parliament, British, 11, 14-15
"Particularists," Whig, 22, 27
Parties, first New World political, 14
Patronage, 61
"Patrons of Husbandry," 104
Peace treaty with England, 21
Pearl Harbor, 155
People's party, 106, 121
Phi Beta Kappa, 57
Philadelphia, Congress in, 17
Phillips, Rev. George, 12
Phillips, Wendell, 73
Pilgrims, The, 11-12
Pinckney, Charles C., 38, 41-42
Pinckney, Thomas, 35
Pintard, John, 31
Pitt, William, 16
Platform, first political party, 63
Platt, Thomas C., 130, 132
Polk, James K., 76-77, 79-80
Poor Man's party, 170
Populist party, 121-22, 125, 128-29, 133
Preamble to the Constitution, 26
President, election of the, 43-44; first not British subject, 70; first U. S., 21, 27-28; proper title for the, 28
"President-maker, The," 54-55
President's House, The, 44, 48
Princeton University, 134
Progressive party, 134-35, 147, 157
Prohibition, 137, 140-41, 143, 148, 151, 153
Prohibition party, 128-30, 137, 170, 173
"Prophet, The," 47
"Prophet's Town," 47
"Proprietary" government, 13
Protestant Reformation Society, 77-79, 83
Public Works Administration, 152

Public works program, 123
Pullman Company, 127
"Pump priming," 152

"Radical Republicans," 100, 102, 105, 108
Randolph, John, 48, 62
Reagan, Ronald, 177
Recession, business, in 1957, 165
Reconstruction Finance Corporation, 151
Reconstruction Period, 99-103, 105, 113, 166
"Red Fox, The," 71
"Red Herring" investigations, 159
"Reds" (Communists), 109, 141
"Regulators, The," 23
Religious intolerance, 77-79, 83-85, 149
"Report on the Public Credit," 31
Republican, Baltimore, 73
Republican elephant (symbol), 110
Republican National Committee, 6, 90, 110-11, 120, 124
Republican Party, 86, 89-91, 93-94, 174
Republicans, 96-97, 100, 104-05, 107, 109-12, 116-22, 124-27, 130-34, 136, 139, 142-52, 154-55, 160-69, 175, 176, 177-78
Republicans, American, 70
Republicans, Democratic, 42, 49-50, 53, 55, 57-58
Republicans, Jeffersonian, 33-35, 38, 46, 48-49, 54
Republicans, Liberal, 107-08
Republicans, National, 58, 60-61, 63, 66, 107
Republicans, "Radical," 100, 102, 105, 108
Revolution, American, 18-19
Reynolds, Verne L., 152
Rhodes, Daniel P., 123
Riots, anti-Catholic, 78-79, 149
Rockefeller, Nelson A., 177
Roman Catholic President, first, 164
Roosevelt, Franklin Delano, 142, 145, 148, 152-56
Roosevelt, Kermit, 133

Roosevelt, Theodore, 130-35
Rooster and crow (symbol), Democratic, 74
"Rough Riders," 130-31
"Royal" government, 13
Russell, Benjamin, 49
Russell, John, 107

St. Augustine's Roman Catholic Church, 78
St. John's School, 17
St. Tammany Clubs, 31
Saltonstall, Sir Richard, 12
Satellite, first artificial, 166
Saunders, William, 104
Scalawags, 99, 101
Schrank, John, 134
Scott, Dred, 94-95
Secession of southern states, 97
Second Continental Congress, 18
Secret Service, U. S., 133, 135
Sectionalism, 53, 60-61
Selectmen, Board of, 13
Senate, 26, 91-92, 138, 180
Shays, Capt. Daniel, 23-24
Shay's Rebellion, 23-24, 150
Sherman, John, 117-18
"Silent Cal," 146
Sirhan, Sirhan, 177
Silver, free coinage of, 122, 126
Sixteenth Amendment, 106
Slavery, 50, 52-53, 72, 79-82, 86-89, 91-98
Smith, Alfred E., 148-49, 151, 168
Smith, Howard W., 6
Smith, William Lloyd, 169
Smithsonian Institution, The, 133
"Smoke-filled room," 143
Social Democratic party, 116, 127-28, 132
Social Democratic Workingmen's party, 99, 110, 113
Social security, 128, 174
Social Security Administration, 153
Socialism, 128, 171
Socialist Labor party, 113, 132, 152, 170-71, 173
Socialist Party of America, 132, 137, 141-42, 148, 151-52, 170

Socialist Workers' party, 171
"Solid South," 103
"Sons of America, The Order of the," 84
South Carolina, secession of, 97
Space race, 166
Spanish-American War, 131
Sparkman, John J., 161
Speaker of the House, 44, 54
"Spoils system," 61-62
Sputnik I, 166
"Squatter" sovereignty, 87
Stalin, Joseph, 156
"Stalwarts," 117
Stamp Act, 14-16
Stamp Act Congress, 15
Stanton, Edwin M., 102, 105
Stanton, Elizabeth Cady, 82-83, 86, 88, 99, 105-06, 121
"Star-Spangled Banner, The," 74
"Star-Spangled Banner, The Order of the," 84
States, order of, ratifying Constitution, 27
States, powers of the, 19
States' Rights party, 27, 157
Stephens, Alexander H., 97
Stevens, Thaddeus, 100
Stevenson, Adlai E., 118, 161
Stock market, 148, 150, 153
Stokes, Carl, 178
Stone, Lucy, 106
Stowe, Harriet Beecher, 87-88
Straight-Out Democratic party, 108
"Strict constitutionists," 33, 45, 53
"Strong Government" Whigs, 22, 26-27
Succession, line of Presidential, 44
Suffrage, woman. See also Women's rights
Sullivan, Charles L., 172
Sumner, Charles, 91-92, 100
Sweeney, "Pete," 114

Taft, Robert A., 160
Taft, William Howard, 130, 133-34
Talleyrand, 38, 45
Tallmadge, James, 52
"Tammanend," Chief, 31

INDEX 191

Tammany, Society of the Sons of, 31, 67
Tammany Hall, 31, 67, 93, 113-14
Tar-a-Ri, 14
"Tariff of abominations," 58-59
Taylor, Glen H., 157
Taylor, Zachary, 80-82, 160-61
"Tea party," Boston, 16
Teapot Dome oil scandal, 144
Tecumseh, Chief, 47-48
Television in politics, 161-62, 164, 168-69, 172-73
Temperance party, 107
Temple Baptist Church, 170
Tenure of Office Act, 102
Term of office, Presidential, 159
"Terrible Siren, The," 107
Texas Constitution party, 172
Third party, first political, 57
Third term, Roosevelt's, 154-55
Thomas, Lorenzo, 102
Thomas, Norman, 152, 170
Thurmond, J. Strom, 157
Tilden, Samuel J., 99, 111-12
"Tippecanoe and Tyler too!," 73, 75
Tippecanoe River, 47
Title for the President, 28
Toree, 14
Tories, 11, 13-16, 18, 21-22
Toringhim, 14
Total Abstinence Brotherhood, 137
Treasury, first Secretary of the, 29
Treaty of Guadaloupe Hidalgo, 80
"Tricky Dicky," 162
Trotsky, Leon, 171
Truman, Harry S., 145, 155-60, 162-63, 166
Tweed, William March, 113-15
Twelfth Amendment, 37, 43
Twentieth Amendment, 152
Twenty-first Amendment, 153
Twenty-second Amendment, 159
Tyler, John, 71, 76

"Uncle Sam," 50-51
Uncle Tom's Cabin, 87
"Underground Railroad," 73
Union League of America, 100

Union party, 97, 100
United American Mechanics, 84
United Nations, 156, 158-59, 173
"United States of America," 18
United Workers of America, 110, 113
University of Virginia, 6
Upshaw, William D., 152

Van Buren, Martin, 62, 64, 68, 70-71, 73, 75-77, 82, 127, 149, 165
Vanderbilt, Cornelius, 106
Vegetarian party, 171, 173
Versailles, Treaty of, 139
Vice President, election of, 43-44; first, 29; succession of, 67
Vietnam, 175, 176, 177
Virginia, University of, 6
Virginia Committee of Correspondence, 15
Virginia Company, The, 11
Virginia legislature, 15-16
"Virginia Plan, The," 25
Volstead Act, 140

Wallace, George, 176, 178
Wallace, Henry, 157
"War Democrats," 97, 100
"War Hawk, The," 55
"War Hawks," 37, 48
War of 1812, 37, 48-51, 57, 75
Ward, Artemus, 5
Warren, Earl, 157
Warren, Joseph, 90
Washington, George, 20-22, 24, 27-31, 33-35, 38, 42, 44, 55
Washington (D.C.) selection of, as capital city, 32
Watts, Connie N., 173-74
Weaver, James B., 116, 121
Webster, Daniel, 59
Weld, Theodore, 87
Wesleyan Methodist Church, 82
Western Reserve University, 123
"Whiggamore," 14
Whigs, 11, 13-16, 18, 21-22, 26, 66, 68, 70-71, 73-76, 80-81, 86-87, 89-90, 94, 96-97, 174

White House, The, 37, 48, 60, 124, 130, 133, 143, 146, 152, 155, 159, 162-63, 165-66
White League, The, 101
Whitney, Eli, 53
Whittier, James Greenleaf, 73
"Wigwam, The," 31
William and Mary College, 29
Willkie, Wendell, 154-55
Wilmot, David, 79
"Wilmot Proviso," 79
Wilson, Ebenezer, 51
Wilson, Henry S., 93
Wilson, Mrs. Woodrow, 140
Wilson, Samuel, 50-51
Wilson, Woodrow, 130, 134-37, 139-40, 156
Winthrop, John, 12

Wirt, William, 63
Women's Christian Temperance Union, 137
Women's rights, 52, 82-83, 86, 88, 99, 105-07, 121, 128, 130, 137-38, 141-42
Wood, Leonard, 142
Woodhull, Victoria, 99, 106-07
Workers' party, 143, 150-51
Works Progress Administration, 152
World War I, 130, 135, 137-38
World War II, 153-57, 160, 162, 167
Wright, Frances, 52
"Write-in" votes, 174

"XYZ" affair, 37, 39

York, Duke of, 13